10/04

W9-BSM-034

Ancestor Hunt

Ancestor Hunt
Finding Your Family Online

Nancy Shepherdson

Franklin Watts
A Division of Scholastic Inc.
New York Toronto London Auckland Sydney
Mexico City New Delhi Hong Kong
Danbury, Connecticut

Photographs © 2003: A. Natacha Pimentel C.: cover bottom left; Adoption.com: 58; Brown Brothers: 14, 61, 62, 72, 88, 90, 98; Christine Florie: cover bottom right, cover top left, 8; Eileen Robinson: cover center right; Family Search: 27; Genealogy.com: 111, 113; Hulton|Archive/Getty Images: 80; Kathy Santini: cover top right, 9; Nancy Shepherdson: 33, 38, 76, 93, 100, 104, 105; National Genealogical Society, Arlington, VA: 127, 128; RootsWeb.com: 40, 44; The Image Works: 16, 29, 69 (Bob Daemmrich), 12 (Topham Picturepoint).

Maps by Bob Italiano: 122; XNR Productions: 63

Please note: All information is as up-to date as possible at the time of publication.

Book design by Molly Heron

Library of Congress Cataloging-in-Publication Data

Shepherdson, Nancy, 1955–
    Ancestor hunt : finding your family online / by Nancy Shepherdson.
    p. cm.
Includes bibliographical references and index.
ISBN 0-531-15454-8
1. Genealogy—Juvenile literature. [1. Genealogy.] I. Title.
    CS14 .S55 2003
    929'.1'0285—dc21

                                                    2002011646

Contents

Ancestor Hunt

Great-great-grandparents

Great-grandparents

Ciarlo/Perugini

Perugini/Eacobacci

Grandparents

Parents

Eacobacci/Oliveto

Oliveto/Florie

Daughter

Daughter

Florie

Florie

Great-great-grandparents

Doolan/Koch

Great-grandparents

Kozlik/Koch

Grandparents

Kozlik/Kehoe

Parents

Kehoe/Santini

Daughter

Santini

1

The Ancestry Mystery:

Are You Related to Someone Famous?

When you start tracking down your **ancestors,** you'll be amazed whom you find on your family tree. Cherie Dustin, a high school senior, found out that she was related to a pioneer woman who fought off an Indian attack all by herself. Susannah Zeveloff, a junior, discovered that her great-grandmother was smuggled out of Russia in a wheelbarrow. Sara Gredler, a college student who started researching her family history in eighth grade, now knows for sure that she is a distant cousin to Prince William of England.

Cherie, Susannah, and Sara are real students just like you. They've just been researching their family histories a little longer than you have. (Anything's longer than the one minute you've been reading this, right?) In fact, every student who will speak to you about family history in this book is a real person! They didn't know any more about **genealogy**—the study of family history—when they started out than you do right now; but you wouldn't

---

The use of actual names of children interviewed for this book has been granted by permission.

For direct connections to links or answers to questions about anything in this book, go to http://*www.awesomeancestors.com.*

Sara Gredler, interviewed for this book, found during her search that she was a distant cousin of Prince William of England.

believe some of the wonderful things they've found, both online and offline, about their family trees.

Do you have people on your family tree who were brave, famous, or just plain fascinating? Yes, you do. Does that surprise you? Well, it shouldn't. If you trace back just ten generations—about 300 years—you are directly related to 1,024 people. That's more than a thousand chances that an ancestor of yours has done something to make you very proud. There are even more possibilities for greatness when you consider the brothers and sisters of all your ancestors. They're all related to you—and their stories can help you understand what makes your family what it is today.

You may even find a rascal or two hiding on your family tree. What if you found out that you were related to a passenger on the *Mayflower*—and then discovered that he was also the first person ever convicted of murder in America? I think you'd still be happy to have John Billington as a member of your family. After all, think of all the great stories you'd have to tell your friends. What if you found out you were related to someone called "No Nose Maggie," who had her nose cut off in a bar fight? Candee Wilde, a high school freshman, heard that story from her grandfather when she started researching her family history for a school project. Candee wishes she had known Maggie. "My grandpa said Maggie was really pretty when she was young and really strong, too," she remembers. "When you know where you came from, you can tell all your friends and be proud."

Knowing your family's history can help you understand yourself better, too. You may learn where you got your curly hair, hot temper, freckled nose, or talent for music. You may find out why your ancestors settled where they did—which could have a lot to do with where and how you live now. You'll understand better why you love to eat certain things and why your family celebrates traditions that are different from your friends' family traditions. You will almost certainly discover strange similarities between yourself and people who lived long ago. You may even uncover secrets about your family that no one has told you. One thing is certain: the past will come to life for you as it never has before.

"After a while, you start to get to know your ancestors and want to know more and more about them," says Cherie Dustin.

You'll discover stories of family members from the past, giving you a glimpse of the life of unknown relatives.

"I'm not bored in history class anymore, because I try to think of what my relatives were living through at the time. It makes you realize that they were real people who suffered and had problems just like us. They were also people who helped make my life what it is today because of what they did in the past."

Solving the Mystery of Your Origins— The Online Way

Even if your ancestors weren't famous, you'll discover that a lot of them were really interesting. Even better, you'll find out that it's fun solving the mystery of your family's past. Once you become interested in genealogy, the formal name given to the study of ancestry and family history, it quickly becomes like starring in your own adventure movie (*The Mummy?*), where the next step could reveal a treasure—or a pit full of snakes.

What might you find on your ancestor hunt? You could find a long-lost relative. One eighth-grade girl found her birth father last year after looking for him online. He was glad to hear from her, and they made plans to get together. On the other hand, you could find a link back to the "old country." High school freshman Samantha Hasratian made contact through the Internet with the president of an Armenian genealogical society, who helped her find her father's birth certificate as well as many cousins she knew nothing about. You can discover generations of your family going back hundreds of years.

You might also uncover family secrets that your family would rather keep hidden. Family history researchers frequently uncover relatives with more than one spouse, with illegitimate children, or with unsavory professions or diseases. Just keep in mind that everything we discover is a part of who our families are—and discovering everything there is to discover is part of the fun.

As you search for your own ancestors you'll find they left many trails for you to follow. You can find clues about them in Social Security records; in birth, marriage, and death records; in telephone directories, tax records, censuses, county histories, and military records; and even in family Bibles and on gravestones. Your relatives may tell family stories that contain valuable hints about your ancestry, and they may have yellowing documents and photographs hidden away in a box or album that will provide other clues. People put together their family histories from all these sources—and you, too, will find them helpful; but until a few years ago, exploring a family tree was a difficult process.

Today, the search for ancestors is faster and easier than it ever has been, thanks to the Internet. Online, there are millions of bits (and bytes) of information about people's ancestors. It's very likely that some of yours are waiting for you online, too. You just have to know where to look. That's the problem. To beginning ancestor

Today, searching for ancestors has become simple with the use of the Internet.

hunters, the large amount of family history information that is available online can be very frustrating. If their full **family tree** doesn't pop up online in the first five minutes, they're outta there. "If I can't find my family right away when there's so much

Help from Heaven?

Are your ancestors really waiting for you, looking over your shoulder from the beyond, hoping you'll find out about them? Maybe yes, maybe no. More than a few family history researchers, though, will tell you about eerie coincidences that couldn't have happened—but did—that helped them find long-lost relatives. Whitney Martinko, a college sophomore who started her genealogy research at age eight, remembers one day when she was so frustrated about not finding a record she wanted at a library that she just grabbed a book off the shelf. Opening it to a random page, she found a relative, then another, then another. All told, Whitney found "tons" of her relatives in that book, which she had never planned to look at. "They were waiting for me," she says today. Are your ancestors waiting for you?

information on the Internet," they think, "they must not be there at all." Not true.

Your relatives are almost certainly on the Internet; they're just hiding. They are waiting for someone with a sense of adventure to figure out where to start climbing the family tree. They want someone who will search for clues, follow trails, and piece together the pattern. They're waiting online for you to find them—and each relative, or each clue, you find will tell you a little more about your family and what makes it click.

The Treasure Map to Ancestor Gold Online

A wise man once said, "If you want to get where you're going, be sure to take a map." The advice applies to searching for ancestors online. You could go off in most any direction and stumble on somebody's ancestors—but will you ever find yours? You will find them if you follow the step-by-step instructions in this book. You'll be guided through your ancestry quest from the simplest search to the more complex. One chapter will be devoted to each search method.

Here are the basic steps to finding your family's history.

1. Asking for answers. Successful quests begin with preparation. Successful ancestor hunts begin by figuring out what you already know about yourself and your family. Then you begin asking questions, like a detective. Who knows the inside story about your family? Members of your family, of course. They can show you evidence that your family grew and evolved before you were around to see it happen. They can take you back to the scene of crime, your birth and babyhood, show you snapshots of your relatives when they were young, and give you documents to back up what they tell you.

They may even, if you ask nicely, spill the beans about some "interesting" characters in your family. Most of your relatives will be delighted that you are interested in learning about where you come from. In this book you'll learn techniques that will help you get the answers you need to jump-start your ancestor search. You'll even learn some polite ways to get away from a relative who wants to talk your ear off.

2. The name of the game. The most basic online ancestor search is by **surname**. That's another word for what we commonly call "last name." Easy, right? Sure, but even here, there are pitfalls to watch out for. Did your family always spell your name that same way? Probably not. My name has been spelled Shepherdson, Sheppardson, Sheperdson, Shepperson, and Shiperson over the past three or four centuries. Samantha Hasratian, the girl who found her father's birth certificate, at first couldn't find anything online. It turned out that her father changed the spelling of his name when he immigrated to the United States. Once she knew that, she found tons of information on his family.

Your surname has probably changed a lot, too, in all the centuries your family has used it. Spellings often got garbled because many people didn't know how to write their own names. So clerks making records just wrote down what they heard—or thought they heard. Think about your surname. If you didn't know how to spell it and had to sound it out, how would you spell it? Write down all the different spellings you can think of now, and put them where you can find them again. You'll need them later.

Also remember that there are a lot more names in an ancestor search than your surname. Every woman who married into your family brought her father's surname with her, so your family search will include those surnames, too. You'll be asking your family to help you find out what some of those names were, along with the dates that go with them, which will help you decide which one of all the "Joseph Smiths" on the Internet happens to be your ancestor.

Once you know which surnames belong to your family, you can begin with the best online sites for surname searches. You'll also find out where to look to find out (maybe) what your name means and (almost certainly) where in the world it came from.

3. Making the right connections. Your cousins are online, too. You probably have never heard of most of them: your second, third, fourth, or farther-removed cousins. One could be your second cousin once removed, another your fourth cousin twice removed. How come you've got so many weird-sounding relations? Everybody does. Let's say your great-grandmother and great-grandfather had six children. All the children of those six children would be cousins to each other. (Think about your own family: The children of your parents' brothers and sisters are your cousins, right?) What's more, all the children of those cousins would be cousins to each other—and cousins of the generation before; and *their* children would be cousins to all the rest. Figuring out the exact relationship between the cousins is difficult, so don't even try. It's not that important. Just realize that you could have a whole basketload of distant cousins in just three generations.

What *is* important is that distant cousins can be extremely helpful in building your family tree. Even better, the Internet gives you a lot of opportunities to reach out to them. You don't even have to know who they are. You can post messages in cyberspace, and sooner or later some of your cousins will find them. Your cousins will post messages, too, that you can answer when you happen to find them. See what I mean by finding treasure online?

4. Pride of place. When your ancestors left records, most of those were collected and stored by local governments, churches, weekly newspapers, and other small organizations. Some of these records are now online; many more are still stored in dusty files. Either way, it can be tough to find them if you don't know where your ancestors lived. The good news is that there's a lot of information online that can help you find the places they called home. There's also help for tracing your ethnic and foreign roots. Special **Web sites** and mailing lists are devoted to specialized guidance in genealogy for those with roots on six of the seven continents: Europe, Africa, Asia, Australia, and North and South America. There are no sites for Antarctica, because no one is known to have been born there yet—one less place for you to search.

5. The proof of the line. Not everything you need for your family history quest is online—yet. Many times, you need to see a copy of a record made during your ancestor's lifetime to be sure who his or her parents and siblings were. You'll want to see copies of birth, marriage, and death records, for instance. You'll also want to see census records, where you may find detailed information about your relatives that was gathered as part of the government's head count of the population. Most such records have not been transferred to cyberspace, but you can find a lot of information online about where they are and how to get them.

6. More places to look. Did your ancestor fight in a war? Was your family rich enough to leave goods to the next generation? Did they own land? Did they pay taxes? Military, legal, and tax records can be jam-packed full of stories about your ancestors' lives. If they fought in wars, they qualified for pension (retirement) pay, but the government wasn't about to give out money to anyone who asked for it. Military and pension files, if you can find them for your ancestors, tend to be stuffed with proof that the fighting men were who they said they were. Those records can give you clearer pictures of their lives both during and after the wars in which they fought.

By leaving possessions behind when they died—or being taxed on them while living—some of your ancestors may also have left behind records of their status in life. A relative of mine left $5,000 behind when he died, which at first didn't really sound like much; but he died in 1902, when $5,000 was worth about the same as $50,000 today. Anyone who owned land left behind another sort of record. The deed to that land tells exactly what piece of the earth your ancestor once owned. Someday, you may even get a chance to walk where your ancestors walked, on land that he or she actually owned.

7. Your name in lights. The last step is to tell the world about everything you have found. Previous generations did it by publishing family history books that would be read by maybe a hundred people. You can tell the whole world by setting up your own home page on the Internet. This is not hard. You don't even have to know anything about setting up a Web page; there are sites that will do it for you. Of course, if you do know HTML, you can individualize and tailor it to your family's own special story.

Are You Related to Someone Famous?

With all the genealogical information available in cyberspace, it is not very surprising that celebrity family trees are out there, too. You can warm up for your own genealogical quest exploring some celebrity family trees. You may even find the surname of one of your relatives—or your own surname.

> **Celebrity family trees:** http://www.genealogy.com/famousfolks
> **Prince William's relatives:** http://www.royalgenealogy.com
> **U.S. presidents' families:** http://www.legacyfamilytree.com/
>   USPresidents/Index.htm

Fair warning: If you have the surname "Bush" on your tree, don't assume you are related to the president. There are many Bush families that aren't. The same thing goes for the surnames Lopez (Jennifer), Combs (Sean "Puffy"), Washington (Denzel—or George), and any other surname that belongs to a celebrity. Unless you can find an ancestor in common—first and last names, all dates matching—you're probably not related; but if you can, you'll have something to brag about.

Really, though, it doesn't matter whether we are related to celebrities, royalty, or presidents. Our own relatives are impressive enough, no matter what they did in life. They lived it—and they gave life to us. The more you learn about your ancestors, the more you'll understand what I mean. André Hunter Courville, a high school junior, already does: "Some people want to meet stars. I want to meet my ancestors."

Chapter 2

Collecting Clues:
What Does Your Family Say?

Who knows the most about your family history? That's easy. Your family does! You can probably remember lots of times at family dinners when your relatives spent hours talking about "old times." You know—things that happened before you were born. Grandmother may love to talk about going to *her* grandmother's house and making *your* favorite gingerbread cookies. Mom may talk about how she and your dad met and fell in love. Grandfather may talk about taking a car trip with his brothers and sisters in the 1940s. When you ask them about "family history," however, they may say, "Oh, we don't really know anything about that!" Don't believe them.

Because you've heard these family stories over and over, you may think you don't know much about your family's history either. You probably let most of them go in one ear and out the other. Unfortunately, your older relatives are not going to be around forever. Someday you're going to wish you had paid more attention to their memories. Once they are gone, their memories will be gone, too, unless you take the time to record them. What's more, if you're going to find your ancestors on the Internet, your family's stories contain some of the best road signs—signs that will point you in the right direction if you know the right way to listen.

"Talking to my grandparents has given me the most information about my family history and a good opportunity to get to know them," says Jessica Crisp, a college student who started asking about her family history in high school.

What if your family doesn't ever talk about the past? Perhaps nobody in your family talks about anything except what's happening right now, preferring to just live life as it comes. Maybe you never see some of your relatives because of a divorce or family fight. Never fear. There are still ways of digging out information about your past. The way your family talks, the way they look, and even the foods they eat could be important clues to your background. Besides, you never know: Your relatives might open up and tell you more than you suspect they will—if you show an interest. Just follow the tips in this chapter to get them talking.

You may find, though, that a few of your relatives just don't want to talk about family history at all. That's all right. Maybe they'll open up after you do some research on your own and show them you are serious.

You may live with only one parent, who doesn't want to talk about the other side of the family. That's okay, too. Most family historians start out working on just one group of ancestors. You can learn a lot by looking for the ancestors of only one parent, and your parent will probably be glad you are exploring the family. Once you get started, your parent may even encourage you to look further and eventually to discover your complete heritage. Just take it slowly. You'll know from your parent's reactions whether beginning to explore the other side of the family is the right thing to do right now.

What if you're adopted? Your adoptive parents may know more about your birth family than you think they do. They may be afraid, though, that if you find your birth parents, you won't value them as much. The key to opening this door is to assure them that you'll always love them as much as you do today. You can also tell them that, just like teens living with their birth families, you'll understand much more about yourself—and appreciate where you are now—once you know where you come from. You may also want to help create a family tree for your adoptive family.

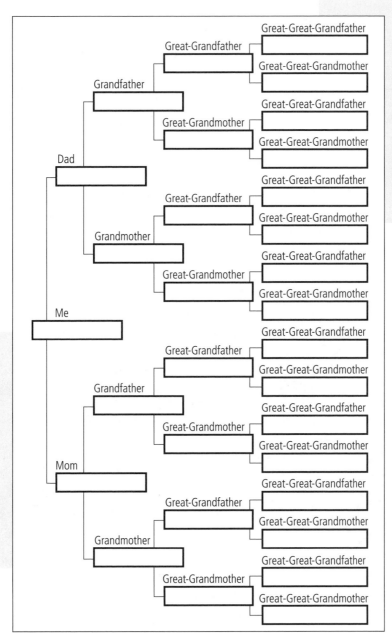

Make a copy of this blank family tree, and use it to build your own personal family tree.

What Do You Know?

Even if you've never explored your family history before, you probably know a lot about your family—much more than you realize. To find out what you do know, you'll want to start filling out a family tree (also called a pedigree chart). You can make a copy of the one that appears on page 25, or you can start building one on your computer. Just go to http://www.genealogy.com and choose "build your family tree."

Whichever chart you pick, fill it in with what you know for sure about your family. Start with your own name, including your middle name, your birthday, and the place you were born. Then fill in the information you know about your parents and grandparents. Do you know who your great-grandparents were? Put them in, too.

Write down every family member's full name, including the middle name, if you know it. If you don't know something, leave the space blank right now. Just putting in "Poppy" or "Nana" and the last name will not be helpful as you start your Internet search. You can also fill out trees for your cousins, aunts and uncles, and other relatives if you like.

Another approach is to fire up a full-fledged software program to keep track of your relatives. A good relative-tracking software program that's free for the downloading is *Personal Ancestral File (PAF)*. To get a copy of your own, go to http://www.familysearch .org, then hit the link for "Order/Download Products" in the upper right of the screen then "Software Downloads." Just select version 5.1 (or whatever is the latest version when you are reading this) and hit the "**Download**" button. This will automatically download *PAF* into your computer so that you can begin entering details about yourself and your ancestors. (If you are using a computer at school or the library, download the *PAF* file to a floppy disk. Ask a librarian or a teacher to help you if you don't know how.)

Begin to explore the software by entering information about yourself. Simply click on the empty box on the upper left side of the first *PAF* page to reveal a form where you can enter your birth date, place of birth, and other details. Hit the "Save" button when you're done. Then click on the drop-down "Add" menu at the top of the screen to enter the information you already know

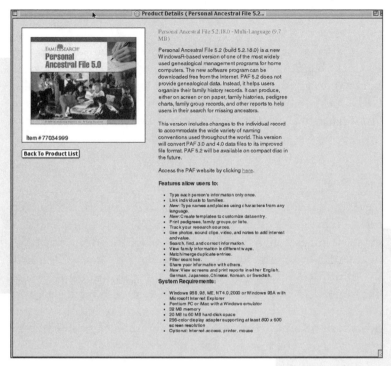

When using the computer on your genealogical quest, the Personal Ancestral File software program is a good way to keep track of your relatives.

about your parents, grandparents, and other relatives. Add Sources (where you got your information—very important) and Notes (stories about each person).

Another good free genealogy software program is *Legacy Family Tree 4.0,* available at http://www.legacyfamilytree.com. The big advantage of this program is that you can view three generations at a time, something you'll appreciate as your family tree grows larger. You can even see the family tree of President John F. Kennedy, which is included as an example. Legacy is a larger program than *PAF* and may take a long time to download if your Internet connection is slow.

If you prefer to buy your genealogy software at a store (or ask for it as a gift), both *Family Tree Maker* and *The Master Genealogist* cost less than $100. (Try *Reunion* if you have a MacIntosh computer.)

At this point, it really doesn't matter which program you pick. All the information you enter into any genealogy program can be transferred to any other program using a file format called **GEDCOM** (more about this later). The important thing is to find a place to keep every bit of information you hear or discover that will help you climb your family tree.

Warning!

Never put anything online that you or your family wants to keep private. That includes phone numbers, names and addresses of living relatives, as well as "family secrets." Anything you put on the Internet can be copied, downloaded to other Web sites, or even sold!

Information posted on commercial family history Web sites like Genealogy.com, Ancestry.com, and ProQuest/Heritage Quest is particularly at risk of being packaged and resold. Never put information about living relatives or family secrets on the Web unless you have permission of the people involved.

Digging Deeper

Now that you've recorded what you know about your family, it's time to start searching for more clues. At dinner tonight or after your homework's done, ask your parents if they can spend a little time with you talking about the families they grew up in. Tell them you are really curious about your family—you are, aren't you?—and just want to hear the stories they have to tell about the past. Once they get over their shock at your interest, they'll probably be delighted to spend some time giving you the facts they know.

If they have busy lives (and who doesn't these days?), make an appointment with one or both of them for a specific day and time. Plan on half an hour or an hour at most, so nobody will get bored. Then post your appointment on the refrigerator for everyone to see. Invite your siblings, too, if they're interested. You may be surprised by what they know, especially if they are older than you.

Asking your parents about the family's ancestors is a great way to begin your search. Bring it up at dinner tonight.

Start with the easy stuff first. Show them your handwritten family tree, or open up your genealogy software program. First ask whether what you've recorded about yourself is right. Ask to see your birth certificate. (Even the parents of adopted kids have birth certificates for their children, although the documents may not list the birth parents' names. If you're adopted, ask to see your adoption papers, too.) Compare the information on your birth certificate with what is recorded on your family tree—what you believe is true about yourself. Every once in a while, people discover that their birth names are not the same ones they are using now. You may even believe that you were born in a different place than you actually were.

Then it's time to ask your parents for their "personal facts."

Record their full names, as well as their dates of birth and marriage. Ask to see their marriage certificate. You should even ask them whether they've been married before, just in case they never told you. Next, ask for your grandparents' full names and their birth and marriage dates. Be sure to ask your parents what they know about *their* grandparents, too. Don't be surprised if your parents don't know all the details, especially about their parents and grandparents. Many people don't know them, especially people who aren't into family history.

You should also ask for the names and birth dates of your parents' brothers and sisters, and their aunts and uncles, as well as the children of all these relatives. If you are using family history software, record this information in your **database**. If you are using a written family tree, use a Family Group Sheet for your parents and both sets of grandparents. (See Appendix A for a copy of the form.) Family Group Sheets have room to write in information about brothers and sisters that your pedigree chart does not. Either way, always remember to ask your relatives to spell any name that's not familiar to you. Was that really "Debuck" that you heard or "Dubuque"?

Once you've got the facts out of the way, then you can start asking your parents for the interesting stuff: what they remember about the family history. Some of the best questions to ask— because they're the questions that lead to stories—are

- Where did you live when you were little? What was it like there?

- What were your favorite foods to eat at home? (Can you make me some?)

- What did you hate to eat? (You hated spinach, *too*?)

- Where did you go to school? What are your best memories of school? Your worst?

- How did you decide what to do for a living? (Do you actually know what they do?)

- How did you meet each other?

- What did your parents do for a living?

- Where did you go on family trips?

I'm sure you'll think of other questions as you talk with your parents.

How are you going to remember everything they tell you? If you write fast, you can take notes, but it's best to use a tape recorder or camcorder, if you have one, to record everything your relatives say. That way, you'll be able to review what was said later so you don't miss anything important. It's so easy to get caught up in family stories that you neglect to write them down at the time, or the people who are telling the stories may get so excited that you can't keep up with them.

Recording family memories on tape is also a great way to preserve them. (Just make sure your equipment is working properly before the big interview day. Don't forget to label your tapes and put them in place where your little brother won't record over them by "mistake.") I wish I had recorded my grandparents' memories. You're lucky if you have living older relatives: They may even remember stories told to them by your great-great-grandparents—the real stories of people who lived more than a hundred years ago.

If your grandparents or aunts and uncles live nearby, ask them whether you can visit them to talk about the family history. Make an appointment, just as you did with your parents, so they'll have time to think about what's most important to tell you. If they live far away and you don't visit often, send them an e-mail or letter asking your questions or ask your parents for permission to call them. You'll probably be surprised at how eager they are to share their knowledge with you.

Playing Detective

You may feel a little embarrassed or awkward, at first, when you're asking questions about family history. This isn't the kind of thing teenagers usually talk about with their parents, grandparents, and other relatives. Think of yourself as a detective hunting down clues or a reporter chasing a good story. In fact, what you are doing is conducting an interview, like the interviews that are shown on television all the time. Here are a few tips that will make your interviews easy—and probably even fun—for everyone:

1. Start with easy questions. Full name, spelling, and dates are questions that get people comfortable with answering "nosy" questions and with speaking into a recorder (if you use one).

2. Prepare a list of questions. Think carefully about what you need to know. Write out your questions ahead of time, but be ready to abandon your list if your interview takes a different, and promising, turn. Don't insist on completing your list of questions if your interview takes you places you didn't know were there.

3. Really listen. In daily life, we tend to spend the time someone is talking thinking of the hilarious remark *we* are going to make next (or worrying about whether our hair's a mess or our clothes look right). Anything but listen to what the person has to say. In an interview, though, you don't have to say anything witty. Make eye contact with the person who is talking, and try to understand every word.

4. Don't interrupt—unless you have to. Do your best not to say anything while the other person is speaking. If you think of a question, write it in the margin of your notebook. If you're taping, you'll kick yourself when you review your tape later if you find that you interrupted just when the story was getting good. However, if your relative gets off the subject too far and shows no signs of coming back to the point after a few minutes, it's all right to interrupt. Wait until the person pauses for a breath, then say something like: "That's very interesting and I'd love to talk about it later, but right now, may I ask you another question about our family's history?" That should get the interview back on track.

5. Pause for a moment of silence. Don't always rush on to your next question. If you feel your family member has not told you the whole story, don't say anything for a minute. Just smile and look expectant. Most people hate silence so much that they will almost rush to fill it with words. What you hear when you use this technique may be the most revealing stories you gather. Try it with a friend you want to tell you a secret. Ask a question, and then don't say anything. Ooh, what you'll hear!

6. Ask to see photos and heirlooms. Ask your relatives to show you the photos and objects that mean the most to them. Your interest in the stories behind them should open a floodgate of memories and stories. Take pictures of the objects if you can, and ask permission to copy your relatives' precious photographs at a nearby copy shop or drugstore. Write the names of the people (with correct spellings!) on the backs of your copies. You'll never remember their names otherwise.

7. Ask for extremes. Get family members in a family history mood by asking questions that make them focus on the most vivid aspects of their memories: "What did you like best about that?" "What did you like least?" "What was the most difficult time for you?" "When were you happiest?" Questions like this will often result in surprising answers.

This is a photo of the author's family in 1916.

8. End politely. Always ask before your interview is over, "Is there anything else you want to tell me about the stories you've shared?" If you know this family member has a lot more family history to share, offer to visit or call again.

9. Be ready for a zinger. When you've put your notebook and recording equipment away and you're ready to go, you're likely to hear the most exciting bit of information you've heard all day. This often happens at interviews, so be prepared for it. Just whip out your notebook and write it down. You'll be glad you did.

10. Relax and have fun!

If you absolutely can't visit or call a relative, send a letter or an e-mail asking specific questions. It isn't fair to write, "Hi, Aunt Martha! Please tell me everything you know about our family's history. By the way, I need it by Friday." Instead, ask a few simple questions in your first letter, and then ask more after your aunt replies. Here is an example of a letter:

Dear Aunt Martha,

I've just started researching our family history, and I'm really excited about it. I hope you can help me by answering some questions.

1. What are the most interesting stories you've heard about our family's past?

2. I'm enclosing a copy of our family tree so far. Can you fill in any of the blanks?

Thanks a lot!

Love,
Sam

Make a photocopy of your pedigree chart or print out a report from your genealogy software, and enclose it with your letter. You might also want to mail a blank audiotape if your relatives have a tape recorder to encourage them to share more memories with you.

CAUTION! Don't Believe Everything You Hear!

What you think you know about your family (and even what your parents say is true) may be wrong. That story about your great-grandfather's being a war hero may be true—but he may have just been a cook in the army. Stories get changed in the telling.

It's like playing the game of Telephone. The more times a story is told, the greater the chance that mistakes will slip in. "When you hear two versions of the same story, don't automatically assume that one is true and the other isn't," warns Ancestry.com columnist George G. Morgan. You'll find out later in this book how to determine whether the "facts" you are hearing really are true.

Also be aware that for various reasons your relatives may want to hide things from you. They may be embarrassed by something they did when they were younger, or they may just feel that it's none of your business. Don't be offended if you find out later that something you were told wasn't true. Just be understanding.

In the interview stage you are simply searching for clues to your family's past. Even if you have already heard a story from Aunt Sally, listen carefully to Uncle Fred's version of the same story. The details may be different, so you should take notes on both versions. That way, you'll have more clues to check out when your search moves to the Internet. The truth is out there, somewhere—or so you hope.

It's a Challenge

Take some time to think about your relatives, young and old. Which one are you most curious about? Great-Uncle Dave who fought in the Korean War? Your grandmother who died when you were little? Now think about who knows the most about that person. It could be the person himself, as in the case of Great-Uncle Dave, who is still very much alive and kicking; or in the case of your grandmother, it might be Aunt June, who lived near her when she died.

Your challenge is to find out all you can about one relative (your "target") from the one person who knows the most about him or her. Here's what you should do:

1. Make contact with the person who knows the most about your "target," which could be the person himself or herself, by phone, e-mail, or letter.
2. Write out a list of questions about the person that you'd like to have the answers to. You may use some of the questions in this chapter, but you should also come up with at least two questions of your own, based on your knowledge of the person.
3. Interview the person by phone or in person. Make a tape of your interview, if possible.
4. Review your tape and notes, and then write up a page or two describing the person and your most interesting discoveries about his or her life to share with your family.
5. Don't forget to record in your family tree any facts that you learned about the person.

Chapter 3

Get a Net:

Is Great-Great-Grandmother Hiding Online?

Okay, let's say you've talked to some relatives, and now you know a lot more about your family's names, dates, and stories. Can you now just type in an ancestor's name on the Internet and have him or her leap out at you? It might surprise you to know that that's pretty likely—if your ancestor has an unusual name and you know where to look.

One of my relatives knew only his grandfather's name when he started searching the Internet for his family history. He typed "Vincent Kaptur" into Google, at http://www.google.com, one of the Internet's best **search engines** (more on search engines below). He was amazed to find that one of the first entries was a patent for a grille that his grandfather had invented for a 1940 GM car. High school freshman Samantha Hasratian simply typed the words "Armenia" and "genealogy" into Google and found a genealogy society in that country. After exchange of a few e-mails, a helpful person at the society volunteered to obtain Samantha's father's birth record and other family documents.

Why Use Search Engines?

A search engine is an Internet tool that allows you to look at a lot of Web sites quickly. Its function is to provide you with a list of

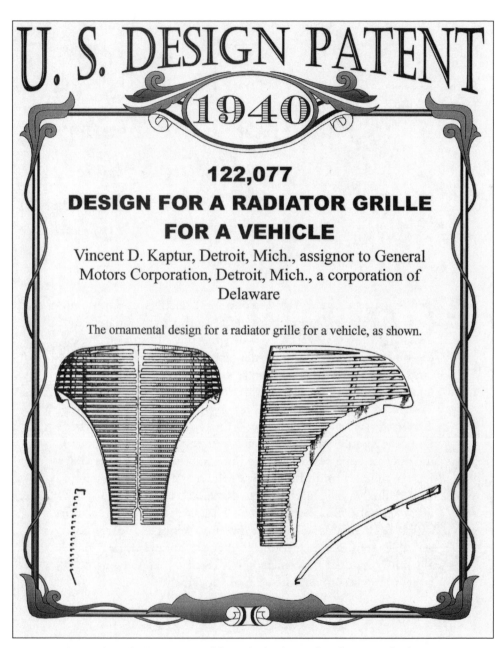

U. S. DESIGN PATENT

1940

122,077

DESIGN FOR A RADIATOR GRILLE FOR A VEHICLE

Vincent D. Kaptur, Detroit, Mich., assignor to General Motors Corporation, Detroit, Mich., a corporation of Delaware

The ornamental design for a radiator grille for a vehicle, as shown.

By searching the Internet one of the author's relatives found a patent for this radiator grille invented by his grandfather.

Web sites that contain the specific terms you want to find. Here are a few other search engines to try:

http://www.altavista.com
http://www.alltheweb.com
http://www.hotbot.com

It's amazing what you can find with a simple search engine search—but can you find your whole family tree back to the Middle Ages, all ready for you to download into your genealogy software program? Sorry, it just doesn't work that way—unless another relative has already done all the research on your family's history and posted it on the Internet. What you will actually find is an almost overwhelming amount of information online that *might* be about the people on your family tree. That's why it's so important to gather names, dates, and stories from your relatives before you start your Internet research. The more you know about your family, the easier it is for you to figure out whether information you find online is about your family or not.

The good news is that it's fun to search the Internet for traces of your ancestors' names. Often you'll find out things you never knew about your family history. Clues you find on the Internet can lead to amazing discoveries.

As a quick first step to see how much information about your relatives is on the Internet, try a Google search for one of the names on your family tree. Pick an unusual name and type both the first and last names into the search box at http://www.google.com. *Very important:* Put the entire name in quotation marks to restrict your search to that name alone. You will be given a list of **links** to Web sites that contain the name. Go ahead and explore any that look promising. Then try another name. Don't type in a name like "John Smith" unless you want to explore the 3,130,000 sites that mention that name!

To see whether your relatives invented anything (1940–1970 only), go to http://www.otterlake.net/antique/antique_patent_gallery.htm, or search the U.S. Patent and Trademark Office for your ancestors' inventions at http://www.uspto.gov/patft.

The Grandfather of Free Ancestor Searches

You can spend a lot of money on searching for your family's surnames (last names) on the Internet. You can buy compact discs (CDs) of births, deaths, marriages, and ship's passenger lists. You can subscribe to genealogy Web pages, but there's no reason to do so—at least not yet—because there are so many terrific free sites to explore.

Perhaps the easiest place to find paths to your ancestors on the Internet is at RootsWeb. This is the oldest and largest free resource for genealogists, with links to hundreds of millions of names. To get an idea how many of your ancestors may be lurking there, go to http://www.rootsweb.com and type one of your family's names into the box marked "Search RootsWeb.com." You can type just the last name if your name is unusual, but you

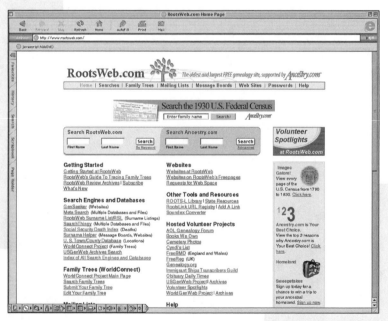

RootsWeb.com is one of the best Web sites to visit when you search for relatives.

should type both the first name and the last name if it is a common name so that you will have a reasonable number of records to examine. (Try typing in "Williams" as the last name to see why: RootsWeb will cheerfully give you more than a million potential matches.)

RootsWeb will search through more than forty databases for your ancestor. You'll find birth, death, marriage, land, census, and military records here for many people. However, RootsWeb may not have records for the part of the country—or world—where your ancestor lived. Don't worry if you can't find much, or anything, about a particular ancestor. It doesn't mean you'll never find anything. We'll look at how to find records of particular localities later. Also keep in mind that no database is perfectly indexed and that the name may be listed under a different spelling than the one you are using. (Try some of the alternative spellings you listed in chapter 1 if you can't find anything about a particular ancestor.)

Spell It Right

Don't give up in frustration if your relatives don't come out of their online hiding places right away. They could be there, with their names spelled differently from what you would expect. Years ago, many of our relatives were illiterate, or at least didn't read and write well. When they told their names to officials who were filling out forms, the officials would spell the names the way they thought they should be spelled. Consequently, census records, immigration documents, birth records, and so on may contain spelling mistakes that make it harder to find your relatives online. Keyboarders working for commercial and volunteer sites may also make mistakes when they transfer information from original documents to Internet databases. Many times, the original documents are almost impossible to read. Did you know that there were no typewriters before 1872? Everything was written by hand before that time, and handwriting was often elegant, even elaborate. Unfortunately, it's often quite difficult to read the fancy handwriting of past years. In addition, some of the documents may have been damaged over the years by age, fungus, or water.

As a result, records your ancestors left behind could actually be on the Internet—but completely misspelled and therefore frustrating to find. The name Hayes could be written as Hays, Hawes, Dawes, Haney, Noyes, or some other variant. Your relatives may also have changed their names, especially if they were trying to blend in with other Americans. I know a young man whose family changed its name from Wolhandler to Handler when they migrated to America. If he hadn't known that, he would have missed a lot of relatives in online databases.

Ask your relatives how your name might have been spelled differently in the past, and remember to experiment with different spellings when you search online databases.

What You'll Find on RootsWeb.com

Spend some time exploring the databases where your ancestors may be hiding. It should become apparent immediately why I recommended that you ask your relatives about the *places* your ancestors were born and died. My grandfather Ernest West was born and died in Illinois. Those records are not indexed on RootsWeb, although they are available elsewhere. Because I know he was from Illinois, I can ignore records from places like South Carolina, California, and Australia. I know I won't find him there. With online genealogy it's often as important to know what to ignore as what to explore.

When you search RootsWeb, the first database that's likely to appear is WorldConnect, which contains family trees that researchers have posted on the RootsWeb site. If you find your ancestor posted on someone else's tree, you have found a distant cousin! Click on the appropriate ancestor name to obtain the e-mail address of your newest relative so you can tell her or him about your great discovery.

Be careful to avoid claiming ancestors that aren't yours. When I was searching for my great-grandfather Presley Williams, I found him among eighteen other Presley Williamses. Knowing when and where he was born and died helped a lot.

You can also post your own family tree—if you are using genealogy software. Look for a function in the file menu that says "Export" and create a GEDCOM file on your C-drive to receive it. Genealogical Data Communications (GEDCOM) is simply a flexible file format. This kind of file allows you to post family trees and share files with other researchers who may not use the same genealogy program that you do. A GEDCOM file will usually end with the extension .ged (for example, YourFamilyName .ged). Once you've exported your GEDCOM to a file, you can then go to http://worldconnect.rootsweb.com (or click the link for "WorldConnect" on the RootsWeb page) and post it yourself.

To submit your tree to WorldConnect, you'll first have to create a user name and password that you can remember. When you add relatives to your tree, you'll want to update your GEDCOM so that more cousins can find you. Then you'll need to enter your name, e-mail address, and a title for your page. Use your last name: "The YourLastName Family Tree." Next, go down to "Upload Options" and browse for your GEDCOM's file name. (All the other options can be left as they are.) Then hit "Upload/Update" at the bottom of the page. People will be able to see your GEDCOM on their searches in twenty-four hours or less. You may even want to send an e-mail to your cousins showing them what a well-connected person you are and asking for more information to fill in the blanks.

As you search WorldConnect, remember that almost everyone who posts a tree is just a regular person like you, not a family history expert. This means you should proceed with caution about inserting information from other trees into your tree, because they may contain errors. You'll need to check out everything you find posted on the Web, using actual records made during your ancestors' lives. I'll show you more about how to do that in chapter 6.

Almost every RootsWeb.com search will also give you matches in the very useful Social Security Death Index. If some of the relatives on your tree have died since 1935, you may be able to find their Social Security records here. Why is this important? In order to apply for a Social Security card, people have to give the government a lot of information, including their parents' full names, where they work, their dates of birth, and where they are living. This information will show you whether the "facts" you've been told by your relatives are actually true and maybe give new ones.

Let's look at a Social Security record to see how this works. Type "Ernest West" into the RootsWeb.com "Search box." Then select "Social Security Death Index." The first entry will look like this:

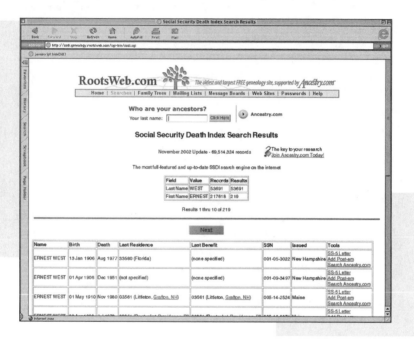

These free records contain a lot of information already: birth date, death date and place, and where the person applied for benefits.

If you are sure one of the people you find was your grandfather or other ancestor (one of them actually is mine) and you don't know much about him, you'll probably want to click the link "SS-5 Letter." This will lead you to a letter you can print out and mail to the Social Security Administration to request a copy of the person's actual Social Security application. The application will contain the names of your ancestor's parents, as well as where he or she was working and living at the time of the application. You must also send a check or money order for $27 along with the letter, so be sure to get your parents' permission (and a check) before you mail the letter. Do not send cash.

High school student Susannah Zeveloff could not find information about her great-grandparents anywhere until she looked at the Social Security Death Index. There, she found them right away. Susannah and her parents sent off for the records and soon she was holding her great-grandparents' information in her hands. "What's best is looking at their signatures and knowing what their writing actually looked like. It makes me feel close to them."

Other Great Places to Look

Another general family history site to explore is Family Search, a site sponsored by the Church of Jesus Christ of Latter-day Saints (the Mormon church). The beliefs of this church make it important to members to locate as many ancestors as they can. As a result, volunteers have spent years transcribing vital records (births, deaths, marriages) in the United States and foreign countries, especially in Europe, England, Scandinavia, and Mexico. Most of these records are for the 1700s and 1800s.

Go to http://www.familysearch.org and click on the photo of the couple who look like grandparents under the "Search for Ancestors" head. Enter a full name in the "Search" box on this page. You'll receive a listing that almost always starts with Ancestral File. You should use these records with caution, since some of the family trees contain mistakes made by volunteers in the early days of genealogy research. Use what you find in the Ancestral File as hints only. For transcriptions of actual records made during your ancestors' lifetimes, look for records listed under International Genealogical Index (IGI) or Vital Records Index (VRI), which are generally more reliable.

If you click on one of these records, you should find a Film Number listed at the bottom of the page. This refers to the microfilm that Latter-day Saints volunteers made of the actual records in which the ancestor appeared. These microfilm records often contain much more information than is listed on the Internet record. For instance, I discovered on Family Search that a relative of mine, Christopher Shepherdson, had died in Yorkshire, England, in 1835. The microfilm of the actual parish death records contained the notation that he was "killed by a fall from a load of straw during a violent hurricane Jan. 7." A "hurricane" in England? Yes, it happened; but I would never have known about it without looking at the original death record.

You can request microfilms containing the records of your ancestors, for a small fee, but you cannot request or view them over the Internet. Instead, you'll need to go to one of many Family History Centers, which are located in Mormon churches around the country. To find one near you, hit the "Library" tab at the top of any FamilySearch.com page and choose "Family History Centers" from the menu at the top of the new page that appears. Type in your state or country in the "Search" box, and you'll bring up a list of centers near you.

You may also want to try searching for your family's surnames at Ancestry.com. You can access this Web page from www

Where Did You Find It?

By now, you may have already screamed with amazement at finding your very own ancestor on the Internet. Could you find him or her again? You could if you printed out the page where you made your discovery. Do that every time, as a first record. You also need to take your record keeping a step further: Write down your source in your family history software. (You've started using a software program, haven't you?) In *Personal Ancestral File (PAF)*, all you need to do is click open the "Info" box on any person and then hit any small "s" in the right-hand column. Other software programs handle sources similarly. Trust me on this: You won't remember where you found Great-Uncle Bert's birth certificate a year from now unless you write it down—now.

.rootsweb.com or www.ancestry.com. About a third of the databases on Ancestry.com are free and worth a look. You'll have to subscribe in order to use the rest unless your public library subscribes. Many do. Check it out next time you're there.

The Best of the Rest

Here's a selection of some more free or low-cost Web sites where you can search for your ancestors by name. In chapters 4, 5, and 6, you'll learn how to find your ancestors by making contact with other researchers and by learning more about the places where they lived and what they did there. For now, the name of the game is names.

1. What's Your Name Mean? The names on your family tree may be clues to where your ancestors came from. If you discover an interesting first name (also called a **given name**)—or if you want to know what your own first name means—go to http://behindthename.com. Here you'll find everyone from Aaron (which means "exalted" in Hebrew) to Zuzanna (the Polish form of Susan). You may be surprised to find out what your name really means and which country it's from. Your ancestors were even more likely than you were to receive given names that reflected their ethnic or religious background or their country of origin. For this reason, given names may be valuable clues in your ancestor hunt.

Finding the meaning of your surname might be harder. Many immigrants to this country changed their names when they arrived. Sometimes immigration officers did it for them, often without their permission, because they couldn't spell the immigrant's real name (as previously mentioned). Weissenberg may have become Weiss or even White. Chien may have become Shen. Names were sometimes translated, too. Faber, Lefevre, and Schmidt all mean Smith, or blacksmith, a maker of metal implements and horseshoes. People with all these names may have become Smiths when they immigrated. To find the meaning of your surname, visit http://www.vitalog.net. This site contains thousands of surname origins from all over the world, including Europe, Scandinavia, Mexico, and Japan. Type in just the first few letters of your name before you hit the "Find It" button so that you can find any name similar in spelling to yours. Or you can type in just the first letter to see every name on the site that starts with that letter.

You can also find many resources about the ethnic or national origins of specific names by typing a surname plus the word "origin" or "genealogy" into a search engine like Google.

2. Find your ancestors' "permanent homes." Obviously, most of our ancestors are no longer among the living. Finding their final resting places can give us their dates of birth and death, as well as lead us to other family members who may be buried nearby. We'll talk more about how to locate cemetery records in chapter 6, but for now you may want to search for your relatives at http://www.findagrave.com. More than 3 million gravestone inscriptions are recorded here; you can search by name alone or refine your search by date or place. (This will be helpful if your name is a common one.) You can also search for celebrity plots here, by name or by "claim to fame."

3. Other places to look—and places to avoid. Be on the lookout for genealogy sites that just want to sell you something. Never buy genealogical information unless you are sure you'll get your money's worth.

One red flag to watch out for is a site that promises to send you your "family crest." Only wealthy families in a few European countries had family crests. Remember, the vast majority of us are not related to royalty, nobility, or famous people. Most of our ancestors were farmers or other working people, because the majority of people who ever lived were. This doesn't mean that our ancestors were not interesting or important people—at least to us, who wouldn't be here without them. It just means that most of them don't have family crests or famous names.

You should also be cautious about any site that seems to promise more than it can possibly deliver. "Trace your ancestry back to Adam and Eve!" We all know that's impossible, right? What about a site that promises that you'll find your ancestors on a CD of the descendants of *Mayflower* passengers? Pretty unlikely, since there were only 102 passengers, half of whom did not survive the first winter.

Another site you should explore is the massive http://www.gengateway.com. Gengateway.com has a surname search similar to the one on RootsWeb, but it also has a variety of "gateways" to unusual databases, such as the U.S. Civil War Center and several African-American genealogy pages, including http://www.Afrigeneas.com. Wherever your ancestors came from, you're likely to find a connection to them through one of these gateways.

Can You Find . . . ?

1. The meaning of your first name? Your last name?
2. The origin of your last name?
3. How many people with your exact name (given name and surname) are listed on RootsWeb.com, FamilySearch.org, and Geneanet.org? How do you feel about this?

Chapter 4

Tell the World:
You've Got Mail!

J osh Taylor was in seventh grade when he found his first relative on the Internet. "I was searching through an Internet message board when I found a posting about a Taylor family that sounded like mine. I responded to the message, and it was my family! The guy who posted the message was a distant cousin of mine who lives in New York. We spent a whole lot of time trying to figure out exactly how we were related," Josh laughs, remembering the excitement of making that connection.

Josh, now a senior in high school, is thoroughly hooked on family history. In fact, he gives lectures on genealogy to both teens and adults. One great thing about posting on message boards, he says, is that no one ever knows how old you are. "They treat you like an adult as long as you act like one." This is not something you can say everywhere you go in the nonvirtual world, right?

Posting messages about your family on **message boards** is like setting up a billboard big enough to be seen from outer space. It lets you shout, "Here I am!" to relatives all over the world. No one may see your message today or tomorrow, but eventually someone looking for your relatives will come across it—and make a connection. Maybe you'll learn about four or five more generations of ancestors, or maybe you'll just find a pal who *may* be related to you. Either way, contacts you make on message boards (and on e-mail lists) can help you when you run into what family historians call a **brick wall**: the relative whom you cannot find out anything about no matter how hard you try. I've knocked down several of those brick walls with the help of people that I met online.

Take that, wall!

"Can You Tell Me Everything About Great-Grandmother?"

You'll get the most help from message boards and mailing lists if you know the right way to post. "Don't ask anyone to send you 'all their files' (on a particular family) or expect your cousins to share what has taken them twenty years to research. They might, but don't expect them to," advises Myra Vanderpool Gormley, certified genealogist and columnist for RootsWeb's *RootsWeb Review.* Most people reading such a message will just move on to the next one. Why? Perhaps because you haven't given enough information for them to know whether they are related to you.

Here's a good example of a message likely to get this family historian some help:

> Subject: SCRUGGS/JONES families, Ohio and Illinois, 20th century
> Hi–
> I'm looking for information about the family of my great-grandmother Eunice SCRUGGS. She was born Jan 20, 1904, in Shaker Flats, Ohio, and died in Elvira, CA, March 12, 1985. She married Emil JONES on June 16, 1925, somewhere in Illinois. Their children were Charles (born in 1926) and Lester, my grandfather (born in 1931), both born in Shaker Flats. Does anyone have a connection to this family on their tree? Does anyone know where in Illinois, Emil and Elvira were married? Any information or suggestions would be appreciated.
>
> Thanks!
> Ted Jones

Writing a message like this gives people reading it enough clues to know whether they might be able to help you—or might even be related to you. They may not have Eunice, Emil, Charles, or Lester on their trees, but they may be related to a Jones family in Shaker Flats or Elvira and may tell you about places to look for more information. On the other hand, they may realize immediately that they are not related to you and not bother you with messages that are not relevant to your search. As you read through message boards and mailing lists you'll learn to love people who write informative messages like this example. Specific messages help you to figure out quickly whether you should keep reading or move on.

Perhaps you don't yet have enough information about your great-grandmother to write a detailed message. This doesn't mean you shouldn't begin to post messages. Just follow a few simple rules to maximize your messaging success:

1. Make your subject specific. In the "Subject" box, include the names for which you are searching, along with places and dates. This is all that people will see as they are browsing message boards. These lists of subject lines are called **threads**. Make your thread as colorful as you can to attract maximum attention.

2. Give as many facts as you can in your message. If you know them, give the full names of the people you are researching; their dates of birth, death, and marriage; and the places where all this happened. These data will tell other researchers whether *your* Emil Jones is the same one as the Emil Jones on their trees. Also keep in mind that people who may not be related to your family could nevertheless have ancestors who lived in the same places. You could make a connection that way and learn more about the places your ancestors lived.

3. Shout it out! Always put the surnames (last names) of your ancestors in ALL CAPS throughout your messages and in the subject line. Usually, you don't want to use all capital letters in an e-mail message because use of all caps on the Internet is considered SHOUTING! Putting the surnames in all caps is an exception because it helps message readers figure out quickly whether your message applies to them.

4. Ask specific questions, if you can. The message writer wants to know whether anyone can tell him where his great-grandparents were married, and he also wants to make new connections he doesn't know about—so he asks about the marriage but also puts out a general invitation for anyone related to contact him.

5. End politely. Always say "thanks!" in advance.

6. Don't give out your age, telephone number, or address. These facts are no one else's business. If someone wants to get together with you for a family reunion or wants to send you something in the mail, tell your parents and get their permission.

Do all this and you will be a master of "Gen-etiquette!"

Hit the Boards

Are you ready to meet your cyber-relatives? The best message board to start with is Genforum, where Josh Taylor found his cousin. Go to http://www.genforum.genealogy.com. This Web site is a collection of thousands of message boards devoted to names, places, and topics in family history. In the "Search" box you may type in any of these terms:

- **Surname**—the last name of one of your ancestors.

- **U.S. state**—either the whole state (California) or its abbreviation (CA).

- **U.S. county**—the full name of the county only (not the state).

- **Country**—the foreign country where your relatives lived.

- **General topic**—for instance, "Vietnam War" or "adoption."

For example, if you type the surname Triplett into the box, the message board for that name appears. Or you can choose a topic.

Once you find a forum that looks interesting, you can search each message one by one, or you can narrow your search by typing something into the "Search This Forum" box. I usually try to choose an unusual surname, given name, or place name that is likely to bring me closer to my own ancestors. I might type "George Washington" into this forum because I know one of my Triplett ancestors, who was born shortly after the Revolutionary War, was named for our first president. This can also bring up a lot of other Georges, Washington county, and messages about the first U.S. president, but at least it gives me fewer messages to sort through.

You may choose to search only the "Latest Messages," "Today's Messages," or the "Last Seven Days." The disadvantage to this is that you may miss some important connections. Messages stay active on Genforum for at least three years, and you should look at the old messages, too. You can reply to any message you see simply by hitting the "Post Followup" button at the end of the message. You may also click on the poster's name and find an e-mail address if you want to send a private message. Of course, you can—and should—start posting your own messages as well. Do this by simply clicking on the "Post New Message" button at the top of each forum page. After you post your message, you just wait for the replies to roll in.

That's the best part of Genforum: You can have the site notify you by e-mail if someone responds to your posting. There is a check box at the bottom of your reply that says "Notify Me Whenever Someone Responds to My Message"; this is a free service. You'll probably also want to check back regularly to see whether anyone has posted anything about your relatives, especially as you learn more about them. To make it easy, go to the very bottom of any interesting forum page and click "Add This Forum to My Genforum." This will create a list of your personal

Hot Tip! Get a Family History E-Mail Address

Your postings will stay on Genforum and other message boards for years, so it pays to use a free e-mail address for your postings. Then even if you use another e-mail address as your main address and if it someday changes, you'll still receive notification from your message boards at your free address. Sign up for one at http://www.juno.com, http://www.hotmail.com, or http://www.yahoo.com and check it regularly.

forums on the Genforum home page. When you return later, you'll need to make only one click to find yourself back among family.

More Message Boards

RootsWeb.com, Ancestry.com, and FamilyHistory.com have recently combined their huge message boards. You'll need to visit only one place to search all of them. You can get to the boards from Ancestry.com, but the RootsWeb.com interface is easier to use: Just go to http://www.rootsweb.com and hit the link for "Message Boards." (You may need to choose a password, but it's free.) On the search page you can search *every* board in this group by typing a name or place into the first box, "Search All Message Boards." You can also find out whether there are boards devoted solely to your family name: "Find a Message Board." If you wish, you can "browse" through the message boards by letter of the alphabet, by location, or by topic. Message topics include **obituaries** (death notices), cemeteries, and adoptions.

If you can't find a message board for one of your surnames or interests, you may start one of your own. Just hit the link called "Request New Board" at the bottom of the page. If there really isn't a board for that name, it will be created, and then you can start posting messages to it. Other people will find it when they perform a search.

Just for Adoptees

RootsWeb also sponsors a message board just for people who've been adopted. You can talk to people about adoption, or you can ask questions. To get there from the RootsWeb Message Boards Home Page, hit "Topics" then "Adoptions." Many more interesting message boards (such as "Old West") are also on "Topics."

Respond to any message by clicking on it. You'll notice that, contrary to what you've been advised to do, many posters (most of whom are adults!) say something like, "I'd be interested in anything you know about my family." Just ignore them. They'll be back when they learn proper "Gen-etiquette." As with GenForum, when you post, you'll automatically be notified by e-mail if you get a response, so use your genealogy e-mail address when you reply.

Great-Great-Grandfather's in the E-Mailbox

Let him out! Seriously, the best clues to your family's origins come from people who are searching for the same last names. They may even be your cousins. Maybe they know where your great-grandmother lived before she moved to California. Maybe they treasure a letter she wrote to her sister talking about her trip out west. Maybe they have a family Bible with her name in it. Before the Internet came into being, it was almost impossible to make contact with your relatives if you didn't already know who they were. Now they may actually write to you. Best of all, your

Get Lots More Messages

Can't find your family yet? You'll find dozens of links to more message boards and e-mailing lists at:

- http://www.cyndislist.com/queries.htm
- http://www.cyndislist.com/mailing.htm
- http://www.gencircles.com

Also, consider subscribing to http://www.rootsweb.com/~newbie for genealogy "newbies" and http://lists.rootsweb.com/index/other/Miscellaneous/GENTEEN.html, a mailing list for teens only. (See page 57 for how to subscribe.)

Remember! Never post anything on a message board about living relatives unless you have their permission.

newly discovered cousins will probably know things about your family that you have never heard before.

To set yourself up to get mail from your new relatives, go back to RootsWeb.com, but this time, hit "Mailing Lists" or type in http://lists.rootsweb.com/. You'll find links there for more than 24,700 mailing lists. As soon as you get there, hit the link to subscribe to *RootsWeb Review*. Read current and past issues on that page or hit "Suscribe" at the bottom. (Just type "subscribe" in the "Subject" box and again in the body of the blank e-mail form that comes up.) It's a weekly e-zine about genealogy, with stories about successful searches and new links to explore. *Lara Croft: Tomb Raider* this is not, but it will pump you up to find out that great discoveries are possible. You'll probably even want to send in an article about your family finds someday. If it's an exciting true story about a family history discovery, *RootsWeb Review* will want to publish it. Your age doesn't matter.

Then go back to the RootsWeb mailing lists page and start looking for mailing lists related to your family. Look for your family's surnames, places of birth or death, or ethnic origins. If you are disabled, you'll even find a list where tips on research aids for you are discussed. Hit whatever link interests you. In the middle of the page, you'll find a link that says something like "Subscribe to SMITH-D" (digest).

Subscribing this way (in what is called **digest mode**) means that all the messages posted to the list on a given day come to you in *one* e-mail message. You can easily scroll through them all, reading only those pertaining to your family search. (Subscribing in **list mode**—for example, SMITH-L—on the other hand, means that all the messages would come to you individually. With some popular lists that could mean hundreds of individual messages a day.)

To respond to a message in digest mode, just hit the "Reply" button as you would normally to answer an e-mail, but be sure to change the subject line of the message to something specifically related to your message. Remember, the more detail, the better. You want your relatives to be drawn to your message, right?

Remember Sara Gredler, who found out in high school that she is a distant cousin of handsome Prince William of England? (See chapter 1.) She suspected it was true after reading the messages on the Strong family mailing list (STRONG-D or STRONG-L). She posted a message about it, and a researcher who was also a subscriber helped her make the connection to her royal family. Tallyho, Sara! Maybe the queen will invite you to tea.

If You're Adopted

Matthew Head used e-mail lists and message boards to find his birth mother when he was in his early twenties. He joined mailing lists on http://www.adoption.com and message boards on http://www.reunite.com. He also registered what he knew about his birth name and birth family at http://www.adoptionregistry.com and http://www.adoptionretriever.com. Eventually he read an e-mail from a woman who was looking for her birth mother in the

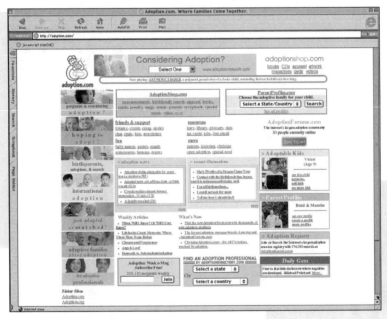

For those who are adopted, http://www.adoption.com can guide you during your search for birth relatives.

same place his birth mother was when he was born. Soon after, he met his birth mother.

If you are in your teens and are searching for your birth parents, you should ask your adoptive parents for help. Make sure they know you'll love them no matter what you find. Your adoptive parents may have more information about the adoption than they have told you, and they may share it if you show you are serious in your search. In addition, the laws of your state may prohibit you from looking for your birth parents on your own until you are eighteen.

You should also approach your birth relatives with loving care. Matthew advises teens: "I think the most helpful thing in my search was maintaining courteous, respectful, and open communication with people that could help me. I always try to maintain contact, give full information, and offer to help with their research."

For more links to adoption sites, message boards, and mailing lists, investigate both http://www.genealogytoolbox.com/adoption.html and http://www.cyndislist.com/adoption.htm.

Post It!

Start spreading the news:

1. Go to a surname message board on www.genforum.genealogy.com and post a message asking for information about one of your ancestors. Make the subject line and message body as detailed as possible, including full names, towns, and states. Click the "Notify Me" button so you'll be told when someone responds to your message.
2. Respond to a message if you see one related to your family.
3. Subscribe to at least one mailing list in digest mode.
4. Get ready to hear from your cousins!

Chapter 5

Tracking Ancestors:
Where Did They Come From?

Did your ancestors come from New York? Tennessee? Mexico? Were they pioneers? Cowboys? Bankers? Slaves? Or did they arrive on a boat or plane from Europe or Asia? Different branches of your family tree may have come from different places—your mom's from one part of the world; your dad's from another. When you interviewed your relatives, they may have told you where the family came from, or your family may have lived in one place for so long that nobody remembers where they lived before.

Whatever you've been told about your family's "home place," you should be able to find out more about it on the Internet. You may even find out that your relatives are wrong about your family's place of origin. Stories passed down through the generations often get messed up.

Nevertheless, what you've heard from your relatives is a good place to start in your search for the places your ancestors lived. When you search by place, you can prevent serious confusion if you concentrate on one family name at a time. Choose an ancestor whose place of origin you think you know to work on first. This chapter will show you how to find out where your relatives came from and what to do after you find out.

Many family members can be traced to Europe, such as the city of Breslau in Germany.

Some relatives lives began in small middle American towns.

Where in the World?

No matter where in the world your ancestor came from, you can delve into that place through Cyndi's List (http://www.cyndislist .com). Cyndi, who is a real person, has collected more than 180,000 genealogy links and put them on this site. You can follow any of these links to discover an almost unbelievable wealth of information about ancestors. To find the country you're interested in, either enter it in the "Search" box on the right-hand side of the main page or browse for it in the alphabetical list of subjects.

Caution: Not all countries are listed individually. Mexico, for instance, is listed under Hispanic, Central and South America, and the West Indies. You can also look on Cyndi's List for places within the United States.

In fact, Cyndi's List includes so many places that it can be a little overwhelming if you don't know much about where your ancestors came from. Before we go any further, a little geography lesson: Perhaps geography isn't your thing, but you have to know a bit about it in order to get very far with family history research. Here's the key: Almost all states in the United States are organized into smaller units called **counties**. (The exception is Louisiana, which is organized into parishes.) Almost all the family history information contained in "place-specific" U.S. family history sites on the Internet is organized by county. You need to know the county names of the places you are looking for in the United States. Outside the United States, genealogy information could be organized according to such governmental divisions as province (in Canada), canton (in Switzerland), department (in France), townland (in Ireland), or rajones (in Eastern Europe).

Pennsylvania's counties

What if you have only a city name and country? How can you find the state, county, or other geographical subdivision you need? First, go to http://www.encyclopedia.com for a brief overview of the place you are interested in. It should be there if it's not a tiny village. If your school or library subscribes, http://www.britannica.com can be a great source of information, too. Look at the first line of the listing in particular, where you'll find that, for instance, Acapulco is in the Guerrero state of Mexico and was founded in the year 1550. If your ancestors lived there, you may be able to find records of their lives going back several centuries. You can also look up your ancestral town on a map at http://www.multimap.com (world) or http://www.mapquest.com (United States).

If your ancestor lived in the United States and you just needed the county name, go to http://Resources.rootsweb.com/cgi-bin/townco.cgi. When you get there, type a city or town name into the "Town Name" box. (You don't have to enter a state name.) You'll soon see a list of all the places in the United States with that name, plus the counties and states they are in. Take the time now to insert what you learn about your ancestor's place of origin in your software or family tree. You'll need this information over and over. Click on the county you just found for lots of facts about your relative's county, at least as it is now. Are cities there? Small towns? What might your relative's life have been like here?

People Who Know Your Places

A huge site called The WorldGenWeb Project, is the next place to look for information about your ancestral home. It is a collection of Web sites created by volunteers from all over the world. The idea is to guide you to the most useful historical tidbits about your ancestor's home place. Many of these sites even have fully searchable databases of historical records that may include your ancestor's name. You may also find birth, death, marriage, and cemetery records. Some sites also have some **census** records typed up and ready to look at. (Censuses are periodic counts of the population, or the people who live in a place. Very few censuses are online yet. Feel lucky if you find one.) The site you find may also include photographs of the area, biographies of early settlers, or links to any number of other places to look for your ancestor. What you will find really depends on what the volunteers in that area decided to post.

For example, if you go to http.//worldgenweb.org and click on the "Country Index" (you'll find it by scrolling down to below the map), you'll see all the WorldGenWeb sites. If you knew that your great-grandfather lived in Adams County, Idaho, you'd click on "USGenWeb" (for all the GenWeb sites in the United States). On the main USGenWeb page, you would next click on "The Project's State Pages," then click on "The Table of States" and pick "Idaho." On the Idaho page, you would click the link for Adams County. Finally, you would have arrived at your great-grandfather's neighborhood.

Although this search for Adams County sounds complicated, it really isn't. All you have done is drill down from the largest geographical division (THE WORLD) to one of the smallest (Adams County). Each time you begin the search for a different ancestor's home on WorldGenWeb, you'll drill down in the same process. As long as you know approximately where a town is from your encyclopedia and map research, you should be able to find it easily in WorldGenWeb. (You can also go directly to http://www.usgenweb.org if you know your ancestor lived in the United States.)

Okay, let's go back to the Adams County, Idaho, page and look for your great-grandfather. The first thing you'll notice on the county page is two columns headed Formed and Parent County. The entries for Adams County in those columns are "3 March 1911" and "Washington." This means that, Adams was carved from a larger county, called Washington, in 1911. When the United States was first settled, large counties were fine because there were so few people in them. As the population grew, it became necessary to reduce the size of the counties to make them easier for local governments to manage.

Why should you care? You'll usually find that where one ancestor set down roots, many others also lived. You may be able, using local records (see chapter 7), to trace your ancestors back several generations. Eventually you may get back so far that the records simply end. Does that mean that your ancestors were living somewhere else and hadn't moved here yet? Not necessarily. It could just be that the county changed its borders and the records are housed somewhere else. Especially when you trace ancestors back beyond 1900 or so, it's important to be certain that the county you are searching in is the correct one for that time period. All USGenWeb sites will tell you when county boundaries changed. Some will even show maps of the historical county lines in various years.

Let's assume, though, that your great-grandfather lived in Adams County after 1911; you can feel confident clicking the link for that county. What you find is a site that offers links to the county's history, queries from researchers, and records that volunteers have posted. Some sites have automated search functions; others require you to search through them manually. Either way, you'll learn a lot about where you come from if you read what has been posted by people who may be your distant relatives. Explore the whole site: You may find great-grandfather lurking here.

What if you don't find anything specifically about your relative? Does that mean he didn't live in Adams County? Not necessarily. The goal of the WorldGenWeb Project is to put all important local records on the Web, but the task began only in 1996 and will take a long time to complete. Most sites today contain only a fraction of the records held by local governments in dusty basements and on microfilm, but more records are being added every day. In fact, you can volunteer to help get them online. Contact the coordinator listed at the bottom of each main page to get involved in helping to put records online. The first thing you'll probably be asked to do is submit transcriptions (typed-out copies) of any documents you have regarding your ancestors who lived in the area. Anything you can do will help, and no one will turn you away because of your age. As your great-grandfather might have said, "Many hands make light work."

You can also help transcribe census records for another project run by USGenWeb. Josh Taylor, who became a census transcriber at age sixteen, coordinates census transcription of five western states for the Web site. Lots of work remains to be done, but you can see whether any of your family appears on censuses already transcribed at http://www.us-census.org./inventory/inventory.htm. to search by state and county. Then volunteer!

Who Lives There?

By now, you've figured out at least one city where your ancestors lived. If the town is not huge and your ancestor's surname is not too common, you may be able to easily hook up with living relatives there. Here's how. Go to an Internet people-finder site, such as http://www.switchboard.com, or http://www.whitepages.com. Type in the surname and the city and state you are interested in.

If you are lucky, several names will show up. Print them out so that you can keep a record of whom you have sent letters to and who has responded. You don't want to bother these people more than once. *Important:* Don't call these people. They may not be interested in talking to you, and it costs money. However, hardly anyone minds receiving a letter from someone who may be a relative, or you can send an e-mail to a relative who has an e-mail address. Hit the appropriate link for finding an e-mail address at either site.

Recently I sent letters to all the Shepherdsons I found living in the area where my father grew up. Almost immediately, I received a reply from a second cousin. He had actually known my grandfather, who died when I was three years old, and had photos of him to send to me. My cousin was very happy to hear from someone on our side of the family; he had thought we were lost forever. We weren't lost, though. We were just waiting for the Internet to help us find him.

Your letter to these possible relatives should be similar to the one you sent out by e-mail in chapter 4. Include as much as you can about the names and the birth, marriage, and death dates of your ancestors who lived in the town. A good ending to your letter would be: "Does any of this sound familiar? If so, please write back to me." It is possible that no one will respond, either because they are not related to you or because they are not interested. Just accept that and move on, crossing them off your list. If anyone does reply, share the letter with your family before you respond. They'll help you make sure the person is really related to you. *Caution:* Don't give out your phone number, and don't mention your age. This information is your own, and you should keep it private business until you find out whether people who reply are related to you and can be trusted. (Your parents can help you to make this decision.)

Connect with Your Ethnic Heritage

Every American family comes from somewhere else. Even Native Americans are descendants of people who crossed the Bering

Ethnic and national origin Web sites can be found that aid in giving information and clues to your heritage.

Strait from Asia thousands of years ago. Some families are closer to their ethnic roots than others. You may know, for instance, that most of your relatives come from China, the Philippines, Mexico, or Africa. The Internet is full of people who are also looking for relatives of your ethnic heritage and who are willing to pass along information and clues to you.

Gengateway.com has a special section called Ethnic Gateway with over a thousand links to Web sites specific to ethnic and national origins. Here you'll find everything from the African American Heritage Preservation Foundation link to the New Zealand Society of Genealogists link. If your ancestors come from Europe, Asia, or the Americas (this includes Native Americans and African-Americans) also check out DistantCousin.com. You can either enter your surnames and search the whole site or explore your ethnic origins at http://www.distantcousin.com/Links/Ethnic. Of course, the mother lode of all list sites, Cyndi's List has a complete listing of its ethnic sites at http://www.cyndislist.com/topical.htm.

Unfortunately, prejudices and customs of earlier centuries have made it harder for some ethnic groups to research their pasts. Here is some extra help for you if your background happens to fall into one of these groups.

■ **Jewish:** In Eastern Europe and Russia particularly, families can be harder to trace because of a tradition of giving the children the mother's maiden name. This lasted in many places until the 1800s. Many Jewish families also changed their names when they came to America. For help with these and other unique challenges, visit JewishGen at http://www.jewishgen.org.

■ **African-American:** Records of slave families often do not exist before the end of the Civil War in 1865, and those that do rarely include surnames because slaves rarely had them. However, the wills of some slave owners provide clues to researchers. You may be surprised to find out that your ancestors were not slaves at all. There have been free blacks in America since the earliest colonial days. For guidance in finding these roots, go to these great sites for African-Americans: Afrigeneas at http://www.afrigeneas.com or Christine's Genealogy Web site at http://www.ccharity.com.

■ **Latino/Latina:** In Latin American countries, the use of the mother's name as part of the surname can be confusing. The Hispanic Genealogical Society of New York aims to cut through the confusion with its Web site: http://www.hispanicgenealogy.com.

■ **Irish:** Many records were destroyed in the Uprising in 1922, but a lot survive, particularly for the 1800s. Genuki (http://www.genuki.org.uk) is the best place to find the most links to both English and Irish databases and sources. For help with research into Irish origins, go to http://www.ireland.com/ancestor.

■ **Italian:** Italian records can be extremely challenging to find because most are not controlled by the government, but by the Roman Catholic Church. However, some have been micro-filmed and are available through the Mormon Church's Family History Centers. For an introduction to Italian family history searching, go to the Italian Genealogy home page: http://www.italiangenealogy.com.

Mayflower, Ellis Island, or What?

If all our ancestors came from somewhere else, how did they get here? This is one of the hardest questions—at least for now—in family history research. Did your family come over with the Pilgrims in 1620? (It turns out that one branch of my family did, although I didn't know it when I first started tracking down my roots.) Did they arrive at Ellis Island, New York, in the early 1900s and leave a full record of their arrival?

Family hunters who are very lucky indeed have a living relative who says something like, "Oh, yes, my parents, my brothers, and I all arrived at New York's La Guardia Airport on American Airlines flight 304 on February 1, 1954." Just as lucky is the researcher who finds a letter or other record in which a more distant relative records the date he or she arrived and on exactly which ocean liner. If your relatives arrived by ship in New York City between 1892 and 1924, you can find them easily, along with the date they arrived and the ship they came in on at http://www.ellisislandrecords.org/search/passSearch.asp.

The vast majority of us, however, will find it very difficult, if not impossible, to figure out exactly how all our relatives got here. This doesn't mean we shouldn't try to track them down. It just means you should remember not to get frustrated if you can't find them—a good thing to remember at many phases of this process. Here are a few good places to look for immigrants to the United States and other countries:

Immigrants arriving in New York City by passenger ship.

- Cyndi's List (http://www.cyndislist.com/ships.htm)
- RootsWeb (http://lstg.rootsweb.com)
- Migrations (http://migrations.org)

In addition, an AOL member has compiled a huge list of passenger list sites at http://members.aol.com/rprost/passenger.html. Ship passenger information is also available at the National Archives and can be obtained through the Mormons' Family History Centers. (See chapter 7.)

Can You Find. . . ?

Find and explore a local site on USGenWeb.org or WorldGenWeb .org where one of your ancestors lived. Did you find anything about your family? If not, what do you know about that part of the world that you didn't know before? Write up two or three paragraphs about what you found out and put it in a safe place. You'll put it to good use when you set up your own home page (it's easy!) in chapter 8.

Chapter **6**

The Value of Offline Searching:
Digging for Proof

Y ou may have started this ancestor hunt hoping that your whole family tree was already waiting for you somewhere on the Net. No such luck, right? It's possible that you haven't yet found *anyone* related to you on the Internet. You probably have found some interesting trails to follow and met some new cousins. You may have even found huge branches of your tree posted by one of your distant relatives. You may even think you've already traced your ancestry back to a king or a famous person.

Is any of what you've found true?

The beauty of the Internet is that anyone can post anything on it—and that's also its problem. André Hunter Courville, a high schooler who has traced his roots back 300 years, warns: "Many people are sloppy genealogists and post mistakes on the Net. Use what you find on the Internet as *clues* to find other sources about your family." In other words, don't accept anything you find there as fact—until you know it's true.

There is only one way to make sure your family tree has all its branches on straight. You must dig for documents that were created during the lives of your ancestors. You'll find their names recorded in old newspapers, historical books, and **vital records** (birth, death, and marriage certificates). You may find these documents in the records of the churches or clubs your ancestors belonged to, or even in the records of cemeteries and funeral homes. It's also very likely that the government recorded your relatives' existence every ten years when it sent census takers out to count everyone in America. (Many other countries have censuses, too.)

Unfortunately, most of the old records you need are not (yet) on the Internet—so how will you find them? You'll look for clues in all the right places and follow them until you track down the people who are related to you. We'll look at the most common ancestral records in this chapter and at more unusual ones in chapter 7.

The Proof in Black and White

Birth certificates are one of the best ways to trace your ancestors. They are the "proof" that you are related to the people you think you are. Most birth certificates list the mother's name, the father's name, and where they were both born. A birth certificate may even have a tiny footprint on it, absolute proof of the baby's identity. (People's footprints never change.) You got a birth certificate when you were born, and you may want to scan it into your genealogy software program. (Most such programs include a way to upload images.)

Marriage certificates can also contain useful information, including the mother's **maiden name**, that is, the surname she was born with. It's usually (but not always) her father's last name. You will find as you continue your genealogy that mothers and other married women can be a bit hard to trace. Especially in the 1800s, many women left records using only their married names, and they may not have had birth certificates. Even so, it is possible to trace many of these women, as some tips in the rest of this chapter will show. If you are lucky, the marriage certificates you find will include a wealth of information about the two people who were married.

Another good source of family history is death certificates. When someone dies, local laws have required (for about a hundred years in the United States, and longer in other countries) that the government be informed about it. These certificates list the reason the person died, which must be filled out by a doctor. A relative or

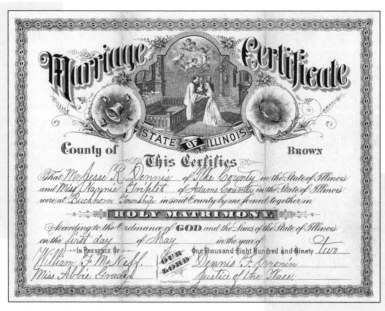

A marriage certificate will provide you with information, such as a maiden name.

close friend is asked to supply the facts about the deceased person's parents, birthplace, spouse, and so forth. Death certificates are often not as accurate as marriage or birth certificates, because the person who really knows the facts—the deceased person—is no longer around, but they can still provide useful clues.

Your parents, grandparents, or other relatives probably have copies of birth and marriage certificates for themselves and also death certificates for other family members. Write, e-mail, or call to ask people who don't live with you for copies of the certificates they have. Here's a sample letter you can use:

Dear Aunt Sally:

Remember that family history project I was working on? [Or tell her about your project if this is the first time you've contacted her.] Well, now I'd like to look at any birth, marriage, or death certificates you have for our family. They will help me prove that everything I have been told is true. I'm asking all of our relatives to help with this. [Then ask her to mail photocopies of certificates she has, or to scan them and e-mail them if she has a computer.]

Thank you, Aunt Sally! Let me know if you are interested in learning what I discover.

Sincerely,
[Your Name]

Type all the information from the certificates you receive into your genealogy program as you receive it; don't let it pile up. When you're done, you'll have a great idea where your family lived for at least a few generations back.

Your Family History in the Courthouse

You don't have to be convicted of a crime to have your name recorded at a courthouse. A courthouse is not just a place where sentences are handed out to criminals. The vital records of the people who were born, got married, or died in each locality are also kept there. A copy of your birth certificate is probably in the files of the courthouse in the county where you were born.

If you know the approximate dates of births, deaths, and marriages, you can have copies of those records sent to you for a small fee. (Ask your parents if it's okay to spend money on this.) You may have learned those dates from talking to your relatives. You can also learn a lot about birth dates from census records, which we'll talk about later in this chapter.

To find the address of the courthouse or government office to write to for your family's records, look up the city or county at the National Association of Counties query board: http://www.naco.org/counties/queries/city_srch.cfm. The link to each county will show you the address of the courthouse in that county (or sometimes the address of another government office). You should write a separate letter for each type of record you request, and not ask for more than a couple of records per letter. Your letter should look something like this:

> County Clerk
> Your Ancestor's County
> Address
>
> Dear Sir or Madam:
>
> I would like to obtain the marriage certificate and marriage application, if available, for my great-grandfather Amos Moore and great-grandmother Lida Grey. They were married on June 1, 1920.
>
> Please let me know how much that will cost, and I will mail you a check.
>
> Sincerely,
> [Your Name]

You will notice that besides the marriage certificate, the letter also requests the "marriage application." This separate document, an application to get a license to marry, may be still in the courthouse files. The certificate itself is issued after the marriage is performed.

You may also buy copies of birth, death, and marriage certificates online through VitalChek (http://www.vitalchek.com). Not all counties participate in this site, but most states do. Even if you don't plan to purchase certificates online, it will be helpful to check here to find out when a state began requiring this type of certificate. If the state you are interested in didn't require birth certificates until 1916, it's not likely to have one for your great-grandfather who was born in 1890. Check out this site before you waste time writing for something that doesn't exist. The site also lists the costs for copies.

Certificates are also sometimes available for people who were born, married, or died in countries other than the United States. Many times, the clerks in those countries will reply even if the letters they receive are in English and that's not their language. For more information on how to locate a foreign records office, visit your country's listings at http://www.worldgenweb.org or http://www.cyndislist.com.

By the way, if you live near the county courthouse where your family's records are, persuade a parent or other agreeable relative to take you there. It's exciting to request an ancestor's record and be handed a copy of it a few minutes later, rather than having to wait a couple of weeks for it to arrive in the mail. It's almost like seeing history coming alive before your eyes.

Counting Noses: The Census Can Tell You More

If you've located relatives born before 1930, you can look at a snapshot of their lives taken every ten years. That's how often the U.S. government takes a census (head count) of everyone who lives in this country. (Foreign countries conduct censuses, too, some of which you can look at. Go to the country you're interested in at http://www.worldgenweb.org for more information.) The last census was taken in the United States in 2000. Did your parents fill out the form?

In the United States, the census has been taken every 10 years since 1790. Since 1850, census takers have listed the names of everyone living in each household, so you'll be able to see your ancestor's parents, brothers and sisters, and maybe even grandparents when you look at the census. Beginning in 1880, the census also listed the birthplace of each person's parents, which is important to know as you trace your family back in time.

Let's start with one ancestor born before 1930 to see how this works. It's easiest to do this if you know the county in which the relative was living in the year of the census. For example, you may know that your great-grandfather Fred Johnson was born in 1917 in a particular county. He would have been about thirteen years old at the time of the 1930 census, so he probably would have been living with his parents; and he would have appeared on the 1920 census as a three-year-old.

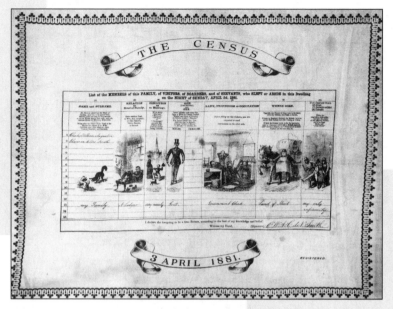

An 1881 UK census lists everyone living in a particular household.

Isn't it strange to think of your great-grandfather as younger than you?

If your town is in the county where your great-grandfather Jones lived in 1920 or 1930, the town's public library may have the right census microfilm just waiting for you to use. Public libraries generally do have census microfilms for their own counties and a large library may have a much more comprehensive collection of census films. The reference librarian can help you, and will probably be happy that you're showing an interest. In addition to the 1920 and 1930 censuses, you may also find census microfilms for the years 1880, 1900, and 1910. In this example, however, you probably won't find what you want from the 1890 census, because most of that census was destroyed in a fire.

If you are close to a good-sized city, you may be able to find all the censuses for every state in your regional branch of the National Archives. To find which of the thirty branches is nearest to you, visit http://www.archives.gov/facilities and hit the link for the nearest state. You must be at least fourteen years old to enter a National Archive branch alone; if you are younger, you must be accompanied by a parent.

If your National Archives branch is too far away and your library doesn't have the microfilm you need, you may request it from your local Family History Center, located in a Church of Jesus Christ of Latter-day Saints (a Mormon church). To search for a center near you, go to http://www.familysearch.org and click on "Find a Family History Center" on the right-hand side of the page. If the center doesn't have the census you need, you can request it for a small fee.

But Where Should I Look?

Millions of people were counted by the census. How in the world will you be able to find the few dozens of individuals related to you? Thankfully, most of the censuses from 1900 on have been fully indexed, and you can look up your relatives by name. (*Note:* The 1880 census index contains only those households with children under ten, and the 1930 census has been indexed for only a few states.)

However, just because there's an index doesn't mean that the census microfilms are alphabetized. That would be too easy, wouldn't it? Instead, you will need to look up each relative's name using a **Soundex** Index. To do this, you have to convert the surnames you want to find into what looks like a secret code, but it's simple once you learn the tricks.

Great-grandfather Johnson's name, for instance, would look like this in Soundex:

J525

Here's how to convert a name to a Soundex code:

1. Write the name down, then cross out all vowels and the letters W, H, and Y (unless one of these is the first letter in the name, in which case you should retain it).
2. Use the first letter of the surname to start the code.

3. Use the Soundex Coding Key to assign a number to each of the next three letters.

Soundex Coding Key

Number	Letter Equivalent
1	B P F V
2	C S K G J Q X Z
3	D T
4	L
5	M N
6	R

4. Stop when you have assigned number codes to three letters. Use zeros if there aren't three consonants in the name.

Weird Extra Soundex Rules to Trip Us Up:

▦ Double letters are counted only once.

▦ If two letters with the same Soundex code are together (like "S" and "C"), only one counts.

▦ Prefixes are either coded or not, depending on how the coder was feeling that day. (Prefixes are combinations of letters such as "La," "D'", "Von" that precede another capital letter.) Try searching for names with prefixes both ways.

A little confusing, huh? Okay, let's try a couple of examples. If we wanted to code the surname Benner for Soundex, we'd first cross out all the vowels and W, H, and Y. (The acronym WHY will help you to remember which consonants to cross out.) BENNER becomes BNNR.

Next, use the first letter to begin the Soundex code, and use the Coding Key to figure out the rest of the code. Did you remember to count the "N"s only once? Then you knew that Benner translates to B560, right? Now, how about Andressen?

Easy, yes? Yes: A536. Were you tempted to start with the "N" instead because I said to cross out all the vowels? Another weird rule: a vowel that starts a name is the only kind of vowel that doesn't get crossed out in Soundex.

Now try translating your own name, and check it using the Soundex generator at http://www.awesomeancestors.com. Sure, we could have told you about this little shortcut at the beginning, but you need to know how to use Soundex if you are staring at a census index and your computer is at home, right?

Okay, I've Got the Soundex. Now What?

Now you need to look for the census index for the right state and the right Soundex for your ancestor. Let's say your great-grandfather Johnson lived in Illinois in 1920. If you remember, his Soundex code is J525, so you'll need the Soundex roll from the 1920 Census of Illinois that contains the "J"s. Be careful to look at the numbers, too. Sometimes a letter code will be on more than one roll. Once you pop your roll onto a reader (a librarian will help if you don't know how), you'll see Family Cards that list all members of a family.

As you scroll through the Soundex looking for Great-Grandfather Fred Johnson, you'll notice not just Johnsons, but also Jamisons, Jimsons, and more. All these names are coded the same way in Soundex because they sound a bit alike. Don't worry about the other names, just look for your relative alphabetically by first name. You may find Fred under the "F"s of course, but you should also look at the Fredricks and Fredericks because that formal name is what his parents may have told the census taker. They may have even used just his initials: F. J. If you don't locate him right away, one reason is that the census taker may have misspelled your family's name. Think of other logical (or illogical) spellings, figure out whether the Soundex code is different for those spellings, and search the Soundex again.

I Found Them on the Soundex!

Congratulations! It can be very exciting to find people you know are related to you staring up at you from the Soundex Index. People three times your age have been known to squeal and do a little

Censuses Online

Many U.S. census images have recently been posted at http://www.ancestry.com. Some of these images are searchable by name, so are much easier to use than microfilmed records. However, you must subscribe to Ancestry.com at its highest rate in order to have access to them. Ask your parents if they are willing to spring for the $129.85 it will cost (per year) so you can save time and effort at the library or Family History Center. Maybe you'll get lucky.

However, some counties have transcribed all or part of some censuses for their localities. You'll find whatever is available posted on county home pages at http://www .USGenWeb.org.

dance—so go ahead. Just don't do cartwheels off the microfilm reader. There are more surprises where this one came from—in the actual census records.

Make a photocopy (if your library has a microfilm copier), or copy all the information by hand from the Soundex card. You especially need to know the county plus the little codes on the upper-right-hand corner. You need the Enumeration District (E. D.), the sheet, and the line to find your relatives. Go to the census microfilms (not the Soundex this time) and find the right state and county. Next, find the roll for the county that contains the right E.D. number. Finally, look through that roll on the microfilm reader until you come to the right sheet number, scroll down to the line number you want—and there they are again! Now you'll see that the census itself contains a lot more information than the Soundex Index cards.

Use Soundex to Help Search Online

Once you know your ancestors' Soundex codes, you can use them on many Web sites to make sure you haven't missed anyone when you search. If the Web site gives you an opportunity to search by Soundex, do so. Some records in every database are misspelled, and this may be your only way to find them.

The Pot of Gold.

Once you've located an ancestor on a census, especially on a census from 1880 or later, you'll know a great deal about this ancestor—address, date, and place of birth, names and ages of his or her children, occupation, nationality, and whether he or she owned a home. Sometimes you will even find out whether your ancestor could read. Take the time to copy by hand or photocopy everything, and be careful to include the information at the top of the page that shows what each column means. Your library may have special forms for use in copying the census by hand—just ask. Since censuses are taken street by street or apartment by apartment, write down the names of some of the people who lived near your ancestors when the census was taken. Married people used to live near their families years ago (which may seem strange now), and so you may eventually find out that some of the neighbors are also your relatives.

Pay careful attention to the birthplaces of people in your relative's household. They may show that the family moved between the birth of one child and the next, which will give you a pretty clear indication of approximately when they migrated. Also remember that people in the same household with different last names may be related. A seventy-year-old woman named Mary Smith could be Bridget Johnson's mother. You should suspect that even more if Bridget also has a daughter named Mary. Years ago, people tended to name their children after relatives much more than they do now.

What If I Want to Look Back Farther?

If you've found your relative in all the Soundex-indexed censuses, you can also explore older censuses. The least confusing way to work is to go back in time, following one relative or one family. All the censuses, starting with the first one in 1790, are indexed in books. Ask the librarian who helped you search for the newer censuses to direct you to the older ones as well. The censuses are indexed by state, but only heads of households were named in censuses before 1850. This means that hunting for your ancestors in early censuses will be more difficult, but it is not impossible.

Did They Lie?

You should collect data on each of your ancestors from as many censuses as you can. You'll soon discover patterns in their movements and facts you never knew. You may also discover that your great-grandmother can't keep the birthplaces of her children straight and seems to age only five years between ten-year censuses. Just like people today, sometimes our ancestors didn't trust the government or wanted to appear younger (or older) than they were. Other errors may have been recorded because whoever was home when the census taker arrived simply didn't know all the facts. Even so, once you have census information, you will have more to work with at the courthouse or the historical society, or even on the Internet.

The Five Steps to Finding an Ancestor in the Census

1. Start with one relative. Where was he or she living at the time of the most recent census in which he or she was counted?
2. Code the last name for Soundex if after 1880 and before 1930.
3. Look in the microfilmed Soundex Index or printed index for the last name, then the first name.
4. Check alternate spellings.
5. Find the right census roll, by enumeration district or township, and then find the line for your ancestor.

A Challenge!

Find at least one record about an ancestor that your family doesn't already have. Here are some possibilities:

1. An actual birth, death, or marriage certificate.
2. A photocopied or hand-copied page from a census with the names of the ancestor's family and neighbors.

As you prepare to meet this challenge, remember that the first step is always to track down the record. If you need help, you can call your public library or town historical society for help.

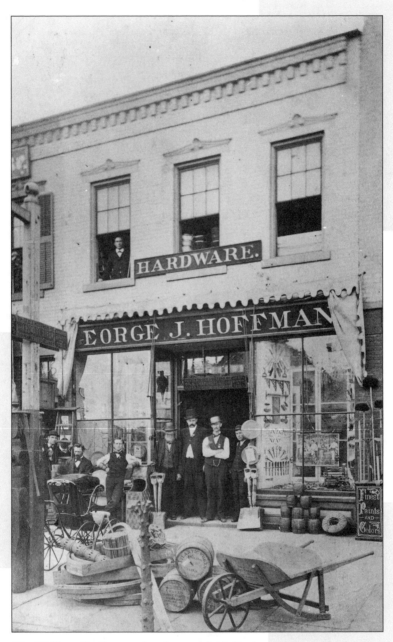

The Hoffman family owned and operated this hardware store in Cleveland, Ohio.

7

Were Your Ancestors Soldiers, Farmers, Rich?
Finding the Threads of Their Lives

Were your ancestors heroes or horse thieves? Rich or poor? Famous, infamous, or anonymous? If you look far enough into your family, you'll probably find people from every level of society. You may find policemen, bar owners, bank owners, or farmers. You'll find black sheep, too, people who ended up on the wrong side of the law.

Whatever details you find, they only add color to the leaves of your family tree. Finding out, as I did, that an ancestor volunteered for three wars gives me a flash of insight into his life. When I found out that the army refused to consider him for a final enlistment because he was too "infirm," it gave me a clear picture of an old soldier who would have done anything to serve his country, whether he could still stand upright or not. Even though this man died in 1904, I feel I know him because I know important facts about his life.

You can find these details yourself, using both online and offline resources. This chapter will tell you where to find some of the most revealing—and interesting—facts.

Money, Money, Money

What your ancestors owned can tell you a lot about them. Perhaps your parents or grandparents inherited a gold watch from an ancestor.

A family in search of a firefighter relative may find clues from this photo taken in New York City, 1912.

Gold was just as expensive back then as it is now, which means your relative had some money. Perhaps your family has antique furniture, clocks, or paintings passed along by your ancestors. Once again, that could mean they were well-off; but be careful: Your ancestors could easily have bought these things at antique stores. If so, the antiques may have nothing to do with your heritage.

The only way to know for sure how much money your ancestors had—or didn't have—is to find out what they owned while they were living. You may have already found out from looking at census records that some of them owned **real estate** (buildings or land), but how do you find out where this real estate was and how much it was worth? There are a couple of ways, all involving courthouse records.

Searching for Deeds

Every time someone buys land (a farm, home, or business), the government keeps a record of the sale, which is called a **deed**. You may personally search deed indexes of grantors (sellers) and grantees (buyers) for property your ancestors owned if you still live in the same area. You can also check FamilySearch.com (http://www.familysearch.com) to find out whether the deed records for that county have been microfilmed. (Click on the "Library" link at the top of the page, then the "Family History Catalog" link, and then the "Place Search" button. Type in the county name and state. Click on the right county, then look for "Land Records." If you find something, ask the Family History Center to request it for you.) Many counties don't yet have microfilmed deeds in the Family History Library, but maybe you'll be lucky enough to find some. I was. I found more than a hundred years worth of land deeds microfilmed for a county in which my great-grandparents owned land.

Most of the time, you'll need to write to the county where the land is located and request a search of their deed indexes. Ask for only one family surname at a time, even if more than one branch of your family lived in the area. You don't want the clerk to refuse your request simply because it will be too time-consuming. (If your relatives lived in a big city and the name is common, limit your request to one ancestor at a time.) When you receive a response, compare the names to your family tree and request copies of deeds of only those people who are related to you. There will be a small charge for making these copies.

Why do you want copies of deeds? For one thing, they often include the occupations (jobs) of buyers and sellers, and their relationships to other people. Land was often sold to relatives, and you may discover relations you didn't know about. In addition, you will get a description of the location of the property. Unfortunately, it won't be a street address. Here's a sample property description:

The North 1/2 of the S.W. Quarter of the S.E. Quarter Section 32, Twp. 16, N.R. 3 W 3rd P. Sangamon County, Illinois.

What? Okay, it seems like a lot of gobbledy-gook, but don't panic. Descriptions like these allow officials to precisely locate the land in question. You should *ask the clerk to mark the location of the property on a map* when you request a copy of a deed. Someday, you may be able to persuade your family to take a trip to see the property. It's really thrilling to stand on land you know your relatives have walked on. I went with my mother to the land described above. As it turned out, the woman who now owns the land went to high school with my father—quite an amazing coincidence.

Did Your Ancestors Homestead?

If you have a relative you think was a pioneer or homesteader, you should look him or her up on a special government Web site. The U.S. Bureau of Land Management keeps records of "land patents" granted to new settlers of the Midwest and the West. Visit http://www.glorecords.blm.gov/PatentSearch/Default.asp to see whether your ancestor is there.

Where There's a Will

When a person dies, his or her property must be given to someone. The person who plans ahead writes a **will,** also called a "last will and testament." It tells everyone how the person wanted the property, called the estate, divided. An executor is appointed to see to it that it is done that way. Most of the time the property goes to close relatives, who are called **heirs**; but this does not always happen. Sometimes close relatives get nothing.

Some people die before they get a chance to write a will. In this case, their property is divided according to the laws of the state in which they were living. This is done by an administrator, and all the property goes to relatives—the spouse and children if they are living.

In either case, the executor or administrator must list everything the deceased person owned (assets) or owed (debts) before the property can be given to the heirs. The good news for you, as a family historian, is that these lists can usually be found in the **probate or administration files** in the county where your ancestor died.

Here's a list of assets I found for one of my relatives:

INVENTORY—Press Print, Griggsville, Illinois.

STATE OF ILLINOIS,
COUNTY OF PIKE.

In The Matter of The Estate of ___William Triplett___ DECEASED.

The following is a full and perfect inventory of all the Real and Personal Estate of said deceased, so far as the same has come to the possession or knowledge of the undersigned _Administratrix_ of _the Estate of William Triplett, deceased_

REAL ESTATE.	VALUE.	
	Dollars	Cents
The south-west quarter of the south-east quarter and the east half of the north-east quarter of the south-west quarter and a strip of land one rod wide, 80 rods in length off of the south half of the south-east quarter of the south-west quarter, all above lands being in section twenty-eight (28)	$2540	.00
The north-east quarter of the north-west quarter and the north-west quarter of the north-east quarter, said last two described tracts of land being in section thirty-three (33) and all of above described lands being in township two (2) south, Range five (5) west of the fourth Principal Meridian in Adams County, Illinois.	$4000	.00
All that part of the south-east quarter of the north-west quarter of section twenty-two (22) lying north of the Wabash Railroad containing nine (9) acres more or less in township four (4) south, Range four (4) west of the fourth Principal Meridian, in Pike County, Illinois.	$1300	.00
Also Lots two (2) and three (3) in Block Three (3) in the original town of New Salem in Pike County, Illinois.	$1100	.00
Also Lots six (6) and seven (7) in Block three (3) in Sargent's addition to the town of New Salem in Pike County, Illinois.	$ 100	.00
Also Lot Number one (1) in Sargent's Sub-Division of the South-east quarter of section fifteen (15) in Township four (4) South, Range four (4) West of the Fourth Principal Meridian Pike County, Illinois, as shown by survey and plat of said Sub-Division made by M. Y. Smith, County Surveyor	$200	.00

No.	CHATTEL PROPERTY.	VALUE.	
		Dollars	Cents
1	horse	50	00
1	buggy	15	00
1	wagon	17	50
4	plows	6	00
1	harrow	2	00
15	bushels corn (estimated)	12	00
1	set work harness	2	00
23	baba hay	8	00
1	saddle	1	50
1	set single harness	3	00
	saws one etc	2	00

What you find, like what I found in Nancy Dennis's probate file, may not sound like much money; but it could have been more than you think. A dollar today is worth approximately ten times more than it was at the turn of the twentieth century. Property worth $500 then would be worth $5,000 now. You'd take it, wouldn't you? For more about how to convert the dollar (and pound and peso) figures you run across in your research, go to http://www.cyndislist.com/money.htm#General.

You'll find will indexes, like deed indexes, in most county administration buildings. Again, you can go to inspect them yourself, look for them on microfilm with a FamilySearch.com search, or request them by mail. Here, too, if you mail your request, don't ask for more than one or two names at a time. It is also helpful to know approximately when your relative died. In some counties the clerks will not search for a probate or administration file unless you know the approximate date of death.

Here's a sample letter requesting such a file.

County Clerk
[Your Ancestor's County]
[Address]

Dear Sir or Madam:

Please look in your Will Index for the probate or administration of the estate of Delbert West, my great-grandfather. He died in 1955 in your county.

If you find any records, please tell me how much it will cost to copy the file.

Thank you.

Sincerely,
[Your Name]

You could also adapt this letter to request information on property transfers by deed.

Once you've read the probate or administration file, you'll have a much better idea how your relative lived. A fellow who died with "one horse and plow" lived a very different life from a man who owned, among other things, "a crystal vase." Keep an eye out, too, for people you've never heard of who receive property in a will or administration. These heirs are almost certainly your relatives, too.

More Courthouse Records

"When you visit a courthouse, be thorough," advises college student Whitney Martinko. Just by asking, she's been allowed to search through dusty records that have revealed a lot about her ancestors, including the fact that one of her great-grandmothers was an orphan who married the son of her guardian at age fourteen. Shades of *Oliver Twist*!

The most revealing courthouse documents are

- Legal files relating to criminal cases and lawsuits.
- Guardianship papers. (This is where Whitney found her orphaned ancestor.)
- Naturalization records. (Judges declared people citizens until the mid-twentieth century.)
- Local tax rolls.
- Voter registration records, if these are public records in the state.

These records, too, can be requested by mail but again, you must limit your requests to one or two per letter. Again, you may want to try to persuade your parents to take you on a field trip to the courthouse where your ancestors' lives were recorded.

Read All About Your Family

A hundred years ago—or even fifty—there were many more newspapers than there are today. Some of the smallest towns had their own newspapers, and they printed things that no newspaper would consider news today: "Miss Hattie Green, a teacher at the grade school, visited her parents in Peoria from Thursday last to Sunday" was big news. Newspapers in small towns—and even big towns—were filled with gossip like this. It was like instant messaging today—except that someone kept a copy. In fact, there is no better place to get a feel for what life was like for your family in past times than old copies of a town newspaper.

The most useful item in an old newspaper is an obituary, which is an announcement of a person's death. Obituaries can contain valuable information about where people were born, what they did for a living, where they died, and who their families were.

Tracking down obituaries can be difficult. There is no central source of newspaper information on the Internet. In addition, many newspapers that our ancestors read—and in which they were written about—no longer exist. First, you'll have to locate the right paper. Then you can write or call the sources listed below to see if they'll look up the obituary for you. Here are some resources to try:

1. The Cyndi's List index of state historical societies and libraries. These facilities may either have copies of local newspapers or know where you should look for them: http://www.cyndislist.com/lib-state.htm#States.
2. News Directory Links lists all the newspapers currently published in the United States, searchable by state at http://www.newsdirectory.com. You can also find magazines and television stations.
3. U.S. county or foreign country sites on USGenWeb.org and WorldGenWeb.org may have listings for either the newspapers themselves or the historical societies that may hold copies.
4. A Google.com search on the town, state (or country), and the word "newspaper" should give you some leads to local newspapers.

If you live near the area where your ancestors lived—or if you visit there—be sure to stop by the local public library and ask to read newspapers from around the dates your ancestors were born, married, or moved to the area. You may find these events either announced or written up in the paper in detail—perhaps with lots of juicy details that will make your ancestors come alive again.

Another place to look for obituaries is RootsWeb.com. If your relatives have died in the past ten years, you may be able to find them in the *Obituary Daily Times* under "Hosted Volunteer Projects" at RootsWeb.com. You'll find the date of the obituary and the newspaper it appeared in when you search on your relative's name. If you're not familiar with the paper, use one of the resources listed above to locate it.

Cemeteries and Funeral Homes

The last resting places of our relatives can be great sources of information for family historians. Dusty files and even the gravestones themselves may contain clues to aspects of your family history that you didn't know. You may also be able to locate a lot of information about your ancestors through funeral records. If you know which cemetery or funeral home your relatives used—and if it is still open for business—call or write a letter similar to your letters to courthouses.

You should ask the cemetery or funeral home employees (by letter or phone call) whether they have any information in their files related to your deceased relatives. You may be amazed at what you find. These places often keep records for a great many years and are usually happy to share information with you, just for the asking (that is, for free).

In addition, volunteers in many areas have gone through the cemeteries, especially old ones, writing down (also called "making a transcription") all the information that is still readable on the gravestones they find.

If you don't know where your relatives ended up (don't assume that your family also doesn't know; make sure you ask them), there are several online sites that can help you find them. Often they contain extensive transcriptions of either cemetery records or the gravestones themselves. George Morgan, "Along These Lines" columnist for *Ancestry Daily News*, published by Ancestry.com, recommends four sites worth looking at:

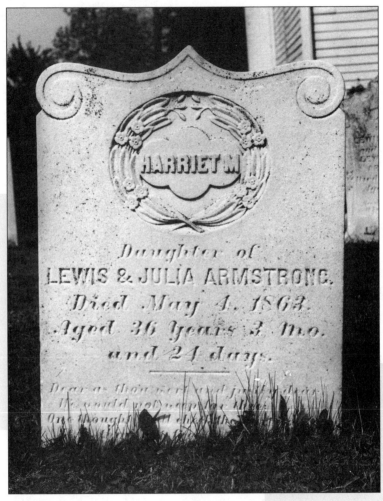

This 1863 gravestone is able to provide valuable information for the Armstrong family.

1. Find a Grave (http://www.findagrave.com) contains, at this time, more than 3.5 million cemetery records from around the United States. Here you'll find the final resting places of celebrities like John F. Kennedy, Jr., as well as millions of ordinary people.

2. GeneaSearch (http://geneasearch.com/cemeteries.htm) has a list of searchable cemeteries both in the United States and in other countries. Not all cemeteries are listed, by any means, but you should check it out.

3. Cemetery Junction (http://daddezio.com/cemetery) lists the addresses of many cemeteries in the United States, Canada, and Australia, as well as a collection of almost 200,000 obituaries from those places.

4. Interment.net (http://interment.net) contains cemetery transcriptions for burial places all over the world.

Local volunteers in the places your ancestors came from may also have made transcriptions of your family's gravestones. Contact the local library or historical society there and ask if they can direct you to these resources, or look up the locality at http://www.usgenweb.org.

If you know the cemetery name but can't find it anywhere, don't despair. You can look up any place name, including cemeteries, at http://geonames.usgs.gov/pls/gnis/web_query.gnis_web_query_form. Just click on "Cemetery" in the drop-down menu for "Feature," type in the cemetery name, and hit "Send Query." Once you receive a result, click on the right county and state, and you'll be able to look at a feature map showing the towns near the cemetery you are interested in. Another approach is to type the name of the cemetery or funeral home into http://www.whitepages.com, and if it's still in business, you'll be given both the phone number and the address.

Ancestors in Uniform

Millions of men—and some women—have served in the military in America and in foreign lands, so it's very likely that you have soldiers, sailors, or other military veterans in your family tree. Some may have been heroes who fought bravely and earned medals. Some may have been leaders; others, lowly grunts who manned the trenches and guns. Still others may have been cooks, clerks, or buglers. Some may even have deserted or been court-martialed. Whatever they did, whenever they did it, there may be records of their military service somewhere. Many of those

Elisha Goodwin West, relative of the author, was 2nd lieutenant, Co. F of the 119th Regiment of the Illinois Infantry. He fought in the Civil War.

records are open to family historians like you, although they can sometimes be a challenge to find.

The first step in tracking down a military record is to figure out what war your relative may have fought in. If your family has told you about relatives who served in the military, start your military research with those people. If not, you need to figure out who might have fought in a war—that is, who was the right age when a war was being fought. Here is a list of wars that should help:

Major Wars Since 1775

1775–1783 American Revolutionary War
1783–1796 Indian wars (United States)
1799–1815 Napoleonic Wars (Austria, Britain, Prussia, Spain, and Sweden versus France)
1812–1814 War of 1812 (United States versus Britain)
1835–1842 Second Seminole War (fought in the U.S. South)
1836 Texas War of Independence (Texans versus Mexico)
1839–1842 Opium War (Britain versus China)
1846–1848 Mexican-American War
1861–1865 American Civil War
1898 Spanish-American War
1899–1902 Philippine-American War
1914–1918 World War I (United States, 1917–1918)
1939–1945 World War II (United States, 1941–1945)
1950–1953 Korean War (United States versus Korea and China)
1961–1975 Vietnam War
1991 Persian Gulf War (United States versus Iraq)
2001 War against Terrorism

Men between the ages of eighteen and thirty are the ones most likely to have fought, but both younger and older men—and women—may have been in the military. *Where* you start looking for military service records depends on *when* your veteran served and *whether* he or she is still alive.

Military Service After 1912

You can probably get a copy of the military record of an enlisted man who served after October 1912 or an officer after June 1917. Here are three reasons I say "probably."

- A fire in 1973 destroyed many World War I and World War II records. However, many of them have been reconstructed, or at least the basic service data are now available. It could not hurt to request your veteran's file.

- If your relative is still alive, he or she will have to request the file and share it with you.

- If you don't have much information about your veteran and he or she had a common name you should provide at least the branch of service (army, navy, marines, air force, coast guard, or reserves) and the birth date. The service number and dates of service would be helpful, too, if you have them.

To request a modern (after 1912) service record, download the military's Standard Form 180 at http://www.nara.gov/regional/mprsf180.html. Fill out both sides as completely as you can, and have your parent who is related to the veteran sign it. Don't worry if you have to leave some of the form blank, but on the front, in section II, number 1, you need to be very specific. Write in (very small): "Please provide all information in his military personnel file including unit orders, awards and commendations, any derogatory information, efficiency reports and ratings, promotion orders, assignment and reassignment orders, photographs, and qualification records." This is the wording recommended by military expert Richard S. Johnson, author of *How to Locate Anyone Who Is or Has Been in the Military,* eighth edition.

Send your Standard Form 180 request to:

National Personnel Records Center
9700 Page Blvd.
St. Louis, MO 63132-5200

Your request will be filled for free in four to five weeks—and then you'll have a wealth of new information about your military relative.

Extra Info About World War I Veterans

If your relative served in the military in 1917 or 1918, he may have been drafted. A special record on these draftees rests in a card file in Georgia. The information includes not only genealogical information but things like hair and eye color, height, and weight. There is nothing like finding out your great-grandfather had the same blue eyes and brown hair you do.

You can scan the file of draftees on Ancestry.com, (http://www.ancestry.com/search/rectype/inddbs/3172.htm) for free. However, not all draftee's records are included, and the file does not include even a fraction of the detail available on the cards. To get a copy of your relative's World War I draft registration card, write to:

National Archives and Records Administration
Southeast Region
1557 St. Joseph Ave.
East Point, Georgia 30344

Soldiers and Sailors Before 1912

Veterans of the Civil War and other nineteenth-century wars live on in their pension files and service records. These files, which

More Military Stuff at Ancestry.com

A great wealth of military databases awaits the researcher at Ancestry.com. Most of them require that you **subscribe** to the basic service for the current fee of $59.95 per year. If your parents don't want to spend that kind of money, check out your public library's adult reference room. Many libraries subscribe to Ancestry.com and allow borrowers to use it for free. Ask your librarian about it.

REGISTRATION CARD

| SERIAL NUMBER | 2930 | | ORDER NUMBER | 22627 |

| rnest | Paul | West |
| (First name) | (Middle name) | (Last name) |

PERMANENT HOME ADDRESS: Augusta Hancock Ill.

| (Street or R. F. D. No.) | (City or town) | (County) | (State) |

Years	Date of Birth		
20	August	Fourteenth	1898
	(Month.)	(Day.)	(Year.)

RACE

White	Negro	Oriental	Indian	
			Citizen	Noncitizen
✓	6	7	8	9

U. S. CITIZEN			ALIEN	
Native Born	Naturalized	Citizen by Father's Naturalization Before Registrant's Majority	Declarant	Non-declarant
✓	11	12	13	14

If not a citizen of the U. S., of what nation are you a citizen or subject? _____

| PRESENT OCCUPATION | EMPLOYER'S NAME |
| Farmer | 17 A. M. Worman |

PLACE OF EMPLOYMENT OR BUSINESS: Augusta, Hancock Ill.

| (Street or R. F. D. No.) | (City or town) | (County) | (State) |

NEAREST RELATIVE	Name	19 W. D. West
	Address:	20 Augusta, Hancock Ill.
	(No.) (Street or R. F. D. No.)	(City or town) (County) (State)

I AFFIRM THAT I HAVE VERIFIED ABOVE ANSWERS AND THAT THEY ARE TRUE

P. M. G. O. Form No. 1 (Red)   03—6171   Ernest Paul West

(Registrant's signature or mark)   (OVER)

This draft card was able to provide the author with helpful information about her grandfather Ernest Paul West.

(Continued on page 105.)

can be huge, record your ancestor's (or his widow's) struggle to prove to the government that he (or she) deserved a monthly payment because of the veteran's service. First, the basic fact that the veteran served at all had to be attested to by people who knew him during the war. His widow would have to prove that they had actually been married and that her children were also his. This was pretty tough in an era mostly before telephones or typewriters and certainly before online databases. One of my

(Continued from page 104.)

relatives did all the necessary work to prove he served and was rewarded with a pension of $12 a month! For this, by the way, he was grateful.

As a result of their efforts, our military ancestors have left behind a wealth of information about themselves. From their pension files we can learn about battles they fought in, officers under whom they served, wounds they received or diseases they suffered from, and the names of their children and wives.

Usually, there are also some surprises. My great-great-great grandfather, for example, threw himself on the government's mercy in his application:

> *[A]s a Calvaryman we landed at Vercruse . . . we was ordered down South after a gurrila cheaf. I am dependent on others than those legally bound for my support for my livelihood; that I have been so dependent since Discharged in Mexico, and that they upon whom I am dependent is Dead + Married. . . . My two eldest sons got married and cannot help and my other three died and now I am depentend on the mercy of the pepal [people].*

From this I found out my ancestor had five sons, three of whom had already died when he applied for a pension in 1887. In addition, I discovered that he could read and write, but not very well, and that he actually saw action in this war.

So, how do you get pension files of your own ancestors? Millions of them are on file at the National Archives in Washington, and you can order them from the comfort of your home if you know:

- The full name of the veteran.
- The military branch he served in (army, navy, marines).
- The state where he entered the service (in towns near borders, investigate both states).
- The war in which he served.
- Whether he served with the Union or Confederate army in the Civil War (see page 107, if Confederate).

You need a special form to request a pension file, called an NATF 85. You can request up to five of these forms at a time, at no cost, at www.archives.gov/global_pages/inquire_form.html. The National Archives will search the files for you (after receipt of the form), also at no charge; but be prepared to spend some money if they find the pension file: Fees for copying each file recently increased to $37 each. Make sure your parents are sitting down when you show them the bill.

Look for Muster Rolls

If you're lucky, you'll also find your relative on a pre-1912 "muster roll" posted online. This is a list that was created when your relative joined a particular regiment and company in the military. It shows promotions, discharges, deaths, enlistment dates, and so forth. Look for muster rolls in his county of residence at http://www.usgenweb.com. You should also look for your state archive's Web site, which may have online databases of muster rolls, especially for the Civil War. To find these records in your state's archive, type in the name of your state, plus the words "state archives military," at http://www.google.com. The site will tell you where to write or visit for a copy of your relative's muster roll. Your regional branch of the National Archives (http://www.archives.gov/facilities) also has mostly complete muster rolls and "compiled military service records" for every war. This may be worth a trip.

If Your Soldier Got in Trouble

Muster rolls and service records also take note of court-martials, desertions, and reprimands. It's likely that the National Archives branch also has a full record of the trial, if the case took place before 1912—another good reason for you to take a trip. Often, the court records show that the soldier had a good reason for, say, deserting. Perhaps his wife was ill and needed help.

If you have an ancestor who was convicted of a crime (or who was court-martialed), don't despair! You can join the Black Sheep Society of Genealogists (http://blacksheep.rootsweb.com) and celebrate his dubious "achievement."

If Your Civil War Soldier Was a Confederate

Johnny Rebs did not qualify for pensions from the U.S. government, so they will not show up in the National Archive files. Many former Confederate states did eventually pass laws to pay them state pensions, however. Your state archives may hold your Confederate soldier's pension file.

Always More to Explore

The more details you find about your family's lives, the more you realize there's always another thread to track down, another clue to follow. That's what's fun about genealogy. You never know where the quest is going to take you or where the next trail is going to lead.

Can You Find. . . ?

Elisha West was twenty-six years old when the Civil War broke out in 1861—just about the perfect age for a soldier. He was living in Camden, Illinois, at the time. Can you find a record of his enlistment in the Civil War? (Hint: use Google.com to search on Illinois State Archives and Civil War.) If you need help, go to http://www.awesomeancestors.com.

Chapter 8

Share It!
Your Family History Home Page

O h, yeah. There's one other thing the computer is awfully good at. When you have a **home page** on the Internet, you can tell the world (and your family) all the interesting things you've discovered about where you came from. You can display your family tree on your home page. You can post a gallery of photos so that everyone can see that your sister has Uncle Harold's big nose—and you have grandmother's beautiful hair. You can put up links directing visitors to other great sites. You can even invite your relatives to the big reunion your family is planning for your close and distant cousins. You can also tell the stories you've discovered about your ancestors—the stories that make your family unique.

The best news is that you don't have to know *anything* about building home pages to build one. All you need to do is go to the Web sites that are waiting to help you do it—for free! Just answer a few questions, and in about ten minutes, you can have a home page of your very own up and running at one of the major family history Web sites. The reason it's so easy is that all the home pages at these sites are put together the same way: plain, no frills. That doesn't mean that these pages are boring. You can display photos, family trees, announcements, and more. You just can't design your Web page any way you please. That's because this kind of home page is constructed using a standard form called a **template.** You just fill in the blanks and—it must be magic—you have a home page.

Of course, if you *do* know a little HTML (the language of Web sites), then you can make your home page even more awesome and artistic.

Once you launch your home page, nobody will know or care that you're younger than most people who have family history home pages. Sara Gredler started her home page when she was thirteen years old. Obviously, it's not as hard as you may have thought it would be to tell the world about your family. Let's look at some of the ways to put together a family history home page, along with some ways to make your page easier for visitors to use. We'll also talk about how to use your Web site to help your family actually pull off that big family reunion.

The Easiest Way: Let the Computer Build Your Home Page

Go to http://www.genealogy.com to look at the simplest free family history home page builder. I used it to construct a home page for one branch of my family, the Armknecht family.

Here's how you can create a home page of your own at Genealog.com:

1. At the top of the Genealogy.com page, you'll see the MyGenealogy.com area. Hit the link for "Create Your Personal Home Page."
2. Fill out your name, address, and e-mail. Be sure to check the little boxes by your name and address saying you don't want this information published on your home page. You should never put this information on your home page. (Also, remove the check marks by the boxes that say you want information by e-mail—unless you *want* your e-mail box to be filled with junk mail.)
3. Name your home page. Choose a title that visitors to your site will immediately understand. "My Super-Great Home Page" may be an exact description, but if you use your family names instead—"The Simpson and Wiggins

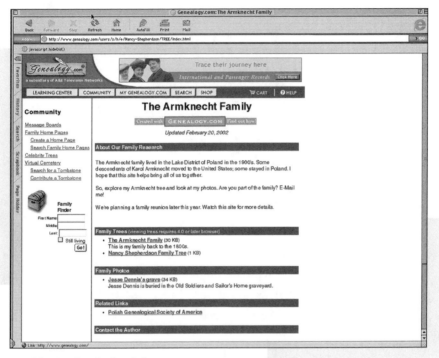

The Armknecht family home page was constructed by the author at www.genealogy.com

Family"—your distant cousins will know in an instant that they've come to the right place.

4. Describe your page. This is where you write the introduction to your page, like the material you see at the very beginning of the Armknecht family page. You can write up to 900 words about your family—almost four double-spaced pages of type—but I wouldn't. People who scan Web pages don't like to do that much reading. Just say a little bit about where your family came from—use your write-up from chapter 5—and perhaps a fascinating fact or two about you. Invite visitors to e-mail you (at your free genealogy account at Juno.com or Hotmail.com), and make sure you sound enthusiastic about wanting to hear from them. Don't worry: You don't have to get everything

exactly right the first time. You can always go back and change anything on your page.

5. Now it's time to begin adding stuff to your page. The first thing is a family tree (or two or three family trees). If you've been using the simple Genealogy.com family tree to record your ancestors, open a window to go to that page, and hit "Share," then "Publish Your Family Tree." Your tree will automatically be transferred to your Web page.

   If you are using genealogical software like *Legacy* or *Personal Ancestral File,* export a GEDCOM file using your file menu. Remember the name of the file you're saving it to. On your Genealogy.com home page, you can **upload** GEDCOM using the "Browse" button under "Family Trees." You'll be asked to give it a title and description so your visitors will know what's in there. Once you've hit "Send," your GEDCOM will be automatically uploaded. Your visitors will see something like the illustration shown on page 113, which is part of the Armknecht Family Tree. (They'll be able to scroll up and down and back and forth to see all of it.)

6. You can add photos to your file if you have them. These need to be in .gif or .jpg files in order to work on your home page. If you know what these terms mean, upload away. If not, ask someone to show you how to use a scanner to create photo files. In addition, you can scan death and marriage certificates as photos, diary pages, notations in family Bibles, and other heirlooms your family lets you borrow.

7. You can add links to any other Web sites you wish, but have consideration for your visitors and make most of the links related to your family.

8. Finally, you can add text files to your site. Have you started writing your family's history? Add it to the page as you get it done.

That's it; you're done—at least for now. You can go back and change your home page any time you get in the mood. Just go back to Genealogy.com and click on the "View Your Saved Home

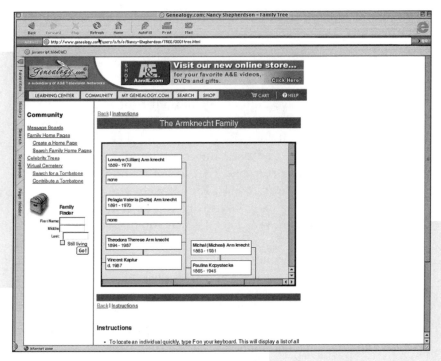

Using genealogical software, you can create a family tree such as this one.

Page" link in the MyGenealogy.com area. Then scroll down to the bottom of the page and click on "Edit Your Page."

More Home Page Builders

A few other home page building methods are worth looking into. Whether you choose one of them depends on your needs, your

---

Crikey, That Was a Big Alligator!

Didn't somebody say it was easy to create a home page? What was all that "go here, go there" stuff? No worries, mate. It takes longer to explain than it does to actually set up your page. So give it a try. Once you get started, you'll have a good day.

software, and your technical abilities. The easiest ones are presented first.

Connect at MyFamily.com

This is the home page builder to choose if a lot of people are already interested in your family's history. All of them can become "members" of your site (for free) and then share news, photos, family trees, stories, and even recipes. Just go to http://www.myfamily.com and type in your name and e-mail address under "Create Your Own Family Web Site." You'll then be asked whom you want to invite to join you at your site. You can fill in the names now or later. (When you do add members, they'll automatically be invited to join you at your site.)

Next, you'll immediately be taken to your new home page, where you can give it a name and start posting. You may also change the features you see on the site (you can delete "Recipes," for instance, if you like) by clicking on the "Site Administration" link on the right-hand side, near the bottom of your home page. Unfortunately, the one thing you can't change is the number of pop-up ads that plague this site.

Use Your Software to Make a Page

If you use certain genealogy software to keep track of your ancestors, you may be able to use it to create Web pages. Among the software packages that allow you to do this are *FamilyTreeMaker* and *Reunion* (for MacIntosh). High school student André Hunter Courville used *FamilyTreeMaker* to create his home page. His family trees, photos, and stories about 300 years of his Cajun ancestors are published on the page. You can see it at http://familytreemaker.genealogy.com/users/c/o/u/Andr-H-Courville/index.html.

Whether you can use your software to set up your own home page is something for you to explore. The next time you are entering data in your software program, look for a button, usually on your top-of-page toolbar, that leads to the Web or the Internet. Often these programs come with many graphic choices that allow you to create an interesting variety of visuals. However, with some of these programs, notably *Personal Ancestral File (PAF)*, all you can do is export a GEDCOM to an existing home page. Check your manual or online help before trying to set up a home page with your genealogy software.

Have It Your Way with HTML: Creating Your Own Web Page

For maximum creativity, you can build your family history home page using Web authoring software like *FrontPage* or *DreamWeaver*. If you know how to use one of these packages to design a Web site, you need to take only one additional step to make it a fully functional family history site: You need to convert your GED-COM into HTML. You can download a program to do this at http://www.cyndislist.com/gedcom.htm. If you want more information on how to construct a family history site from scratch, you can find all the detail you would ever need at Cyndi's Genealogy Home Page Construction Kit (http://www.cyndislist .com/construc.htm).

If You Need Free Web Space

If you create your own home page, you'll need a place to store your information. If your family already has a Web site for something else, you may be able to store your Web page with the same *host* (a company that provides Web space). Otherwise, sign up for a no-cost Web space account with a host like RootsWeb.com, Geocities.com, or Tripod.com. (Note: with RootsWeb, you can't upload your GEDCOM directly, but you can link your home page to a WorldConnect tree. See chapter 2 for more about setting one up.)

What Makes a Home Page Inhospitable

Make it easy on your visitors. They won't waste their time trying to navigate a Web site that's hard to use. Here are some things that are sure to *drive them away*:

- **Dark or complicated backgrounds**. Colors and wavy lines may be cool, but can you read the words on the page? If your site gives you a choice, compare several backgrounds and choose the one that's easiest to read.
- **Animated graphics**. Things that jump around on the page are fun to watch, but they're distracting to people who just want to look at your impressive research.
- **Anything that takes a long time to load**. Many visitors won't wait for things like Java applets, music clips, and slide shows, jazzy though they may be—and they tend to crash older systems.
- **Out-of-date information**. If you change e-mail addresses, don't forget to change your site. Also, regularly check any links you include on your site to make sure they are still working.
- **Mysterious locations**. There are at least nine Springfields in the United States, not including the one where "The Simpsons" live. If you talk about "the Smith family from Springfield" on your home page, visitors won't know which Springfield you mean. Include the county and state when you mention a U.S. location on your site, and include country if the location is outside the United States. Don't just mention these specifics in one place. Using search engines, visitors could be brought to almost any location within your site. Let them know what you're talking about no matter where they end up on your site.
- **It Does Not Work!** Have some friends or relatives try to get into your site. Does everything work right? Is it easy to use? If not, be a pal and make it better.

What Should I Not Put on My Home Page?

- Stuff about your other interests or sports. Stick with your family's history.
- "Facts" you don't know for sure are true. If something is

just a family story, be sure you say that—until you can prove it!

- Photos of people who are still living—unless you get their permission.
- Addresses or phone numbers of living relatives—including your immediate family.
- Images of birth certificates. A criminal could use them to create a new identity for himself or herself.
- Your personal e-mail address, unless you have your parents' permission.
- Anything you don't want the whole *world* to know.

Tell the World

A great home page isn't worth the time it took to put it together unless people you're related to come to visit it—but how can you tell them about it if you don't even know who they are? There are four easy ways:

- **Make sure your opening paragraph attracts search engines.** People searching for your family history on the Net are likely to try a search engine first, as you did in chapter 3. The opening paragraph of your home page should include the words that will draw the attention of those search engines. Always include the words "genealogy" and "family history" as well as several of the names in your tree, along with the different ways your name has been spelled in the past. You could also refer to geographic locations. You could say: "Welcome to the Smith Family History home page. We are exploring the genealogy of the Smith, Wagner, and Bach families, along with Smythe and Bachman. Most of our ancestors lived in Pennsylvania and in Yorkshire, England."
- **Submit it to family history Web sites.** You can ask the owners of other Web sites and home pages to create links to your home page. At http://www.cyndislist.com, for instance, there is a link a little way down the page that

says "Submit a New Link." Hit that and you'll be asked to type in your universal resource locator (**URL**) (which follows http://). Fill in the rest of the blanks, and Cyndi will almost certainly add your home page to her list. Amazing, huh? You can also ask the owners of home pages devoted to your family name to include a link to your site on their pages. Just e-mail the owner, whose address is usually at the bottom of the page, and ask. Include your URL in your e-mail.

■ **Submit it to search engines.** Rather than waiting for a search engine to find you, you can ask that your URL be listed on their sites. Search engines like Google.com, Yahoo.com, AltaVista.com, Lycos.com, and HotBot.com all allow you to list your home page for free. Sometimes you have to look around a bit to find the right place to submit it. At Google.com, you find the right place by hitting the link "Jobs, Press, & Help." You can also submit your home page to fourteen search engines at http://www.addme.com.

■ **Post it to family history mailing lists and message boards.** "Message boards and mailing lists are wonderful places to let people know about your new home page," advises Juliana Smith, editor of the *Ancestry.com Daily News*. She recommends including your URL with your signature in every e-mail you send to a genealogy mailing list or message board. (See chapter 4.) Announce your new site everywhere you can; just include your URL in all your messages and invite people to visit.

Web Sites Are Useful for Offline Fun, Too: Have a Family Reunion!

You can use your home page to invite distant (and close) cousins to a family reunion. Once you've made contact with ten to twenty relatives, talk to your parents about planning a reunion. A picnic in a local park or a group visit to ancestral places is a great way to get to know cousins you've only met on the Internet.

Make sure you plan activities such as family tree sharing for the genealogists in your clan and games for people who aren't really interested in family history. It's safe to say that everyone will enjoy meeting distant branches of the family tree and getting to know how much you all have in common.

A Challenge

Go to one of the sites where you can create a free home page and get one started. Keep track of how much time it takes. I'll bet it won't take long.

Chapter 9

Happy Trails!
Having Fun with Your Ancestors

Now that you know the basics of family history researching online, you could spend all your time staring at a computer screen, looking for one more ancestor: "Not now, Mom! Can't you see I'm hunting for ancestors!" What's the fun in that? Remember, your ancestors were real people with real lives. They danced, they joked, they had a good time. Your research into their lives should be more like play than work—or else why do it?

The main thing is not to get too serious about any of this. Think of it as a hunt for buried treasure, a quest for the keys to a mysterious locked room. Every clue you find takes you a little closer to the truth, a little closer to scoring a goal. "It's like playing a game," says André Hunter Courville. "You want to know everything, so you have to figure out where to look."

If there was such a thing as a genealogy team, the coach would tell you that the best plays are often hidden in plain sight and that you have to use cunning and instinct in order to see them clearly. Sometimes you just have to relax and have fun. Here are some tips to help make the family history game go your way:

1. Celebrate your ancestors' birthdays. Get a good-sized calendar or date book, and write all of your family's birthdays in it, in a bright color. As you find new ancestors, add them to your date book. Pretty soon, you'll have something to celebrate almost every day. Chances are you will—sooner or later—find an ancestor who shares a birthday with you. Put an extra candle on the cake and have an extra piece!

2. Imagine a life. Your ancestors' lives were more than just names and dates. As you research their comings and goings, you'll begin to form pictures of them in your mind. Whenever you have some free time—or want a break from searching—write a paragraph or two about the childhood and teenage years of an ancestor you've learned something about. Find out what was happening during this person's life by reading about local history on http://www.worldgenweb.com or by visiting a history site like http://www.ourtimelines.org. Think about what your ancestor may have been thinking and feeling in response to historical events. Then go a little farther into his or her life. Eventually, you'll be able to turn your jottings into a portrait of the name in your genealogy program, and you may want to write several such portraits. You can distribute them to your family via your Web site, by e-mail, or in booklets for gifts.

You may even want to do the same thing about yourself. "Make it easier on your great-grandchildren: Write down what's happening to you so they'll know about you when they want to do family history," suggests high school senior Cherie Dustin. "I write something about my life at least weekly, if not more often—what I'm thinking and what I feel. I wish my grandpa had done that, since he died before I got to know him."

3. Travel through time. If you can't travel to your ancestral places, buy a big map of the United States—or the world—perhaps at a yard sale or flea market or ask your parents if they have one you can use. Mark on the map the location and the dates of residence of each ancestor for whom you have that informtion. Then imagine you were there with your ancestors. Why would your ancestors have moved when they did? How did they meet their husbands or wives? Did they marry someone who grew up next door, or did they travel a long way to meet one another? Do a lot of your family lines come from the same place? What does that mean for the traditions you have today?

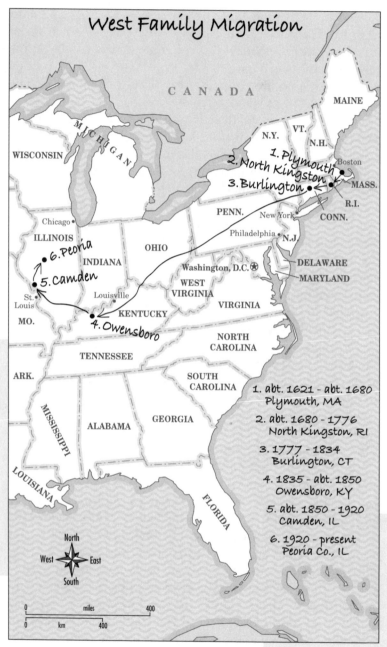

West Family Migration

CANADA

MAINE

WISCONSIN

MICHIGAN

N.Y. VT. N.H.

1. Plymouth
2. North Kingston
3. Burlington

Boston

MASS.

R.I.

CONN.

New York

ILLINOIS

Chicago

PENN.

Philadelphia N.J.

6. Peoria

INDIANA

OHIO

5. Camden

Washington, D.C.

DELAWARE

MARYLAND

St. Louis

Louisville

WEST VIRGINIA

VIRGINIA

MO.

KENTUCKY

4. Owensboro

NORTH CAROLINA

TENNESSEE

ARK.

SOUTH CAROLINA

1. abt. 1621 - abt. 1680
   Plymouth, MA

2. abt. 1680 - 1776
   North Kingston, RI

MISSISSIPPI

ALABAMA

GEORGIA

3. 1777 - 1834
   Burlington, CT

4. 1835 - abt. 1850
   Owensboro, KY

LOUISIANA

FLORIDA

5. abt. 1850 - 1920
   Camden, IL

6. 1920 - present
   Peoria Co., IL

North
West   East
South

0   miles   400
0   km   400

Tracking your ancestors migrations is a fun way to enhance your search.

122

"Time travel" lets you see connections among your ancestors that you might not have noticed before. Of course, real travel can be even better. Your parents (or grandparents) may not need too much prodding to take you to some of the faraway places your family came from. After all, it's their family, too.

4. Pick your favorite. As you've probably already discovered, with even a little research you can find many people who are related to you. This means you will accumulate piles of paper—in your room, on your desk, on your floor—as you print out all the information you find. It can result in terminal confusion, too, for you will soon forget who is related to whom and who lived where. Besides, you know your parents will eventually blow a gasket about all the junk you are piling up—unless you can turn them into ancestor hunters, too.

The easiest way to solve this problem is to concentrate on one surname at a time, or even one ancestor at a time. Find out all you can about that surname line or that ancestor before you move on to someone else. That way, you can search through all the places we've suggested and not miss anything because you were off chasing another ancestor's trail.

Here are some other good ways to tame the paper tornado:

- **Do a little at a time.** Each time you find a bit of info, enter it in your genealogy software program. You *are* using one by now, aren't you? If not, review your options in chapter 2, and also consult some of the resources listed at the end of this book in the For Further Reading section.

- **Keep a log book.** Like the captain of the *Enterprise* in *Star Trek,* you should record where you've explored for each ancestor so you won't forget and do it all over again. Trust me, you will forget if you don't keep a log. See Appendix B for a form you can copy to help you easily keep track of your research trails.

- **Don't pile, file.** Create a notebook for each branch of your family, using a three-ring binder with transparent sleeves to hold your documents. You could also use plastic document holders or plain 10-by-13-inch manila envelopes. The important thing is to have a separate container for each branch of the family. This way once you've entered a record in your genealogy software, you can file it away where you can find it again. (Then the dog won't eat it—or use it as a newspaper!)

5. Avoid the traps. It's easy to lose your focus on the hunt, especially when you search online. Unfortunately, there are also lots of people out there who only want to sell you something. Here's one safe principle that you should always keep in mind when you're surfing for ancestors: *Don't click on any ads.* The only function of some of these is to collect your e-mail address for the purpose of sending you more ads. Most of what you will see advertised—such as census records—can be found offline for free.

Another important principle: Please don't believe any site that claims you are related to Adam or Charlemagne or, heaven forbid, Zeus. The first two lived before family records were kept, and the third is a Greek god! Even so, some people are absolutely convinced they are related to these historical figures because they found it on the Internet. Remember, the Internet gives you clues about your family and trails to investigate. It does not prove anything: You have to do that yourself.

6. Know where to find the coach. When everything fails and you've hit a brick wall, don't give up. Instead, go online and ask questions. The people you meet online are almost always willing, even eager, to help as long as you don't ask: "Could you find my family tree for me?" Here's where to go when you need help:

- **Dear Myrtle.** Hundreds of articles on family history topics fill this site, http://www.DearMyrtle.com, most written by genealogy expert Pat Richley. Find specific topics by hitting "Search" to the right of the drawing of Dear Myrtle at the top of the screen.

- **Dancing skeletons.** The motto of this site, also known as RootsWeb Guide, is, If you can't get rid of the skeleton in your closet, you'd best teach it to dance. There are hundreds of guides here (http://rwguide.rootsweb.com), all waiting to dance an answer to your questions.

- **The Web site for this book.** All the links mentioned in this book are posted at http://www.awesomeancestors.com.

There are also downloadable copies of the forms in the Appendices, as well as new sites for you to explore. I'll even answer specific questions by e-mail, although I cannot do genealogy research for you.

Always Remember: You Are Important to Your Family's History

When it comes to family history, you have a vital role to play. Years from now, your family will be immensely grateful that you spent the time to write down your grandparents' stories—and saved those old letters—and preserved the family's photographs, complete with names and birth dates. Someday, your great-grandchildren will say, "I'm so glad we have these records from the twenty-first century that tell our family's stories"—and you'll be the one who saved your family history for future generations.

As you research your family history and work on fun activities to get to know your ancestors better, you'll start feeling a connection with the people who came before you and will come after. Your family is really no more or less than a chain of relationships in which you are a link. You will become a very important link if you preserve the history of those who went before you and pass it along to those to come in the future.

Family history research also gives you a chance, as you've probably discovered by now, to strengthen your relationship with family. The strongest bond we have is the bond with family—and the more we know about each other, the stronger the bond can be.

Studying family history has probably made history class a lot less tedious for you, too. When you know that your ancestors lived through the times you're studying, it makes them so much more real. Sure, immigration was important to the settling of the United States, but doesn't it become more exciting when you find out that someone related to you participated in it? Your genealogical exploration can make it easier to imagine what it was like to live through each era of history.

Just remember that you'll never find all your ancestors online. No one will ever put every record you need on the Internet.

The amount of information you'll find online will always be tiny compared to what can be found in county courthouses, libraries, archives, and the like. You should always pursue as many avenues of research as you can in your search for ancestors—and now you know where to look. Online research is only the beginning, but with the clues you find on the Internet, you can grow an incredible family tree.

Find Your Awesome Ancestors!

All the teens who participated in this book agreed on one thing: Once you get started, family history grabs hold of you and won't let go. You may do a little now and put it away for later; or you may get involved in a big way, like Josh Taylor, who runs several Web sites, teaches family history to adults, and has been written about in newspapers for his genealogy exploits. Even he once thought that family history was only for adults with nothing better to do. "I always thought history was boring, but this just flashed on me," he says. "I got bitten by the bug."

That's the way it is with these awesome ancestors of ours: The more we know, the more we want to know. In addition, there's always the chance that we'll find out we are related to somebody rich and famous. Maybe Prince William, Bill Gates, or a president is hanging out somewhere on your family tree. You'll never know unless you keep hunting. When you do find your cousin, the president, say hello for me.

If you ever need help or find broken links in this book, click on www
.awesomeancestors.com.

Appendix A

National Genealogical Society	Husband's Code _____
Family Group Sheet	Wife's Code _____

HUSBAND'S NAME: _____

Date of Birth: _____ Place of Birth: _____

Date of Death: _____ Place of Death: _____

Present Address or Place of Burial: _____

Father's Name: _____ Mother's Maiden Name: _____

Marriage Date this Husband and Wife: _____ Marriage Place: _____

Was there Another Marriage: By Husband: ☐ By Wife: ☐ Divorced: ☐ ☐ When: _____

WIFE'S MAIDEN NAME: _____

Date of Birth: _____ Place of Birth: _____

Date of Death: _____ Place of Death: _____

Present Address or Place of Burial: _____

Father's Name: _____ Mother's Maiden Name: _____

Other items of interest about this couple: _____

No.	Children (Birth Order)	(on) Birth Information (at)	(on) Death Information (at)	(on) Marriage Information (to)
1.				
2.				
3.				
4.				
5.				
6.				
7.				
8.				
9.				
10.				

Researched By: *Research Date:*

Address:

Reprinted with permission from the National Genealogical Society.

Appendix B

Reprinted with permission from the National Genealogical Society.

Glossary

Ancestors: Your parents' grandparents and all the grandparents who came before them.

Brick Wall: An ancestor for whom you cannot find parents, despite a great deal of effort; brick walls often fall when we discover new sources of information.

Census: A count of the inhabitants of a certain area; usually includes other information such as sex, age, occupation, and other personal details.

County: A local governmental unit in charge of courts; property taxes; wills; elections; and records of births, marriages, and deaths; most U.S. states are divided into counties.

Database: A collection of related items of information, typically searchable by keyword.

Deed: A document that transfers ownership of land with or without buildings.

Digest Mode and List Mode: Formats in which to receive e-mail from online mailing lists. Digest mode gathers each days' messages into one e-mail message; List mode forwards each e-mail separately.

Download: Receive files from someone else's computer into your own.

Family Tree: A chart showing the relationships between members of a particular family.

Forum: *See* Message Board.

GEDCOM: A file format that allows users of a variety of genealogy software programs to share information; stands for Genealogical Data Communication.

Genealogy: The study of family history.

Given Name: First name.

Heir: Someone who receives a gift of goods, real estate, or money from a person who has died.

Home Page: The first page of a Web site. Also, a simple Web site.

HTML: Abbreviation for hypertext markup language, the language used to create Web pages.

Keyword: A word that you want to find on a Web page or in a database.

Link: A pathway from one Web page to another. Links on Web sites are underlined or highlighted in some way.

List Mode: *See* Digest Mode.

Maiden Name: A woman's surname (last name) before her first marriage.

Mailing List: A group of people interested in a particular subject who receive e-mails from each other. All messages posted to a mailing list are received by everyone on the list.

Message Boards: A Web page where you can post e-mail messages permanently, usually about a specific subject. Also called a **Forum**.

Obituaries: An article about a person's life, printed shortly after his or her death, in a newspaper or other publication.

Probate or Administration Files: Records of the distribution of property of a person who dies with a will (probate) or without one (administration). Usually, those files can be found in county courthouses.

Real Estate: Land and buildings.

Search Engines: An online tool that allows you to find the Web sites containing the specific terms you want to find. For example, http://www.google.com is a search engine.

Soundex: A special index that groups records based on names that sound alike.

Subscribe: Join a mailing list.

Surname: Last name.

Template: A fill-in-the-blanks form that is used to create a simple home page.

Thread: A series of e-mails on a particular topic, posted to a message board or mailing list.

Upload: Sending files from your computer to someone else's computer.

URL: The address of a Web site. Typically begins with http://. An abbreviation for uniform resource locator.

Web sites: A group of related Web pages, owned by a person or group, accessed by a single URL.

Will: A document that states how a person wants to distribute what he owns to loved ones; also called "last will and testament."

Vital Records: Information about births, marriages, and deaths.

Bibliography

Courville, André Hunter. Interview, January 2002.

Crandall, Ralph (Dr.). *Shaking Your Family Tree: A Basic Guide to Tracing Your Family's Genealogy,* 2nd ed. Boston: New England Historic Genealogical Soceity, 2001.

Crisp, Jessica. Interview, February 2002.

Dustin, Cherie. Interview, February 2002.

Flinn, Cherri Melton. *Genealogy Basics Online: A Step-by-Step Introduction to Finding Your Ancestors through the Internet.* Boston: Muska and Lipmann Publishing, 2000.

Gormley, Myra Vanderpool. "Welding Links: Where Have All the Manners Gone." *RootsWeb Review.* http://e-zine.rootsweb.com.

Gredler, Sara. Interview, November 2001.

Hasratian, Samantha. Interview, February 2002.

Head, Matthew. E-mail interview, January 2002.

Johnson, Richard S., Lt. Col. *How to Locate Anyone Who Is or Has Been in the Military,* 8th ed. San Antonio: MIE Publishing, 2001.

Krug, Steve. *Don't Make Me Think: A Common Sense Approach to Web Usability.* Indianapolis: QUE Publishing, 2000.

Martinko, Whitney. Interview, February 2002.

Morgan, George. "He Said, She Said: What to Do with Conflicting Stories." *Ancestry Daily News.* http://www.ancestry.com/library/view/news/articles/dailynews.asp

"Naturalization Records." National Archives and Records Administration. http://www.archive.gov

Rose, Christine, and Kay Germain Ingalls. *The Complete Idiots Guide to Genealogy.* New York: Alpha Books, 1997.

Smith, Juliana. "Clues for Successful Interviews." *Ancestry Daily News.* http://www.ancestry.com/library/view/news/articles/dailynews.asp

Taylor, Josh. Interview, January 2002.

Wilde, Candee. Interview, January 2002.

Zeveloff, Susannah. Interview, February 2002.

For Further Reading

General Family History

Crawford-Oppenheimer, Christine. *Long-Distance Genealogy.* Crozet, VA: Betterway Publications, 2000.

Croom, Emily Anne. *Unpuzzling Your Past Workbook: Essential Forms and Letters for All Genealogists.* Crozet, VA: Betterway Publications, 1996.

Everton, George B. *The Handybook for Genealogists: United States of America,* 9th ed. Logan, VT: Everton Publishers, 1999.

Luebking, Sandra H., ed. *The Source: A Guidebook of American Genealogy.* Orem, VT: Ancestry Publishing, 1997.

Rose, Christine, and Kay Germain Ingalls. *The Complete Idiot's Guide to Genealogy.* New York: Alpha Books, 1997.

Taylor, Maureen A. *Uncovering Your Family History through Photographs.* Crozet, VA: Betterway Publications, 2000.

Internet Genealogy

Flinn, Cherri Melton. *Genealogy Basics Online: A Step-by-Step Introduction to Finding Your Ancestors through the Internet.* Boston: Muska & Lipmann Publishing, 2000.

Hahn, Pamela Rice. *The Unofficial Guide to Online Genealogy.* Hoboken, NJ: John Wiley & Sons, 2000.

Hinckley, Kathleen. *Locating Lost Family Members and Friends: Modern Genealogical Techniques for Locating the People of Your Past and Present.* Crozet, VA: Betterway Publications, 1999.

Richley, Pat. *The Everything Online Genealogy Book.* Avon, MA: Adams Media, 2001.

Special Interests in Genealogy

Colletta, John Phillip. *They Came in Ships: A Guide to Finding Your Immigrant Ancestor's Ship.* Orem, VT: Ancestry Publishing, 1998.

Grenham, John. *Tracing Your Irish Ancestors,* 2nd ed. Baltimore: Genealogical Publishing, 1999.

Herber, Mark D. *Ancestral Trails: The Complete Guide to British Genealogy and Family History.* Baltimore: Genealogical Publishing, 1998.

Johnson, Richard S. Lt. Col. *How to Locate Anyone Who Is or Has Been in the Military,* 8th ed. San Antonio, TX: MIE Publishing, 2001.

Kavasch, E. Barrie. *A Student's Guide to Native American Genealogy.* Westport, CT: Greenwood Publishing, 1996.

Krug, Steve. *Don't Make Me Think: A Common Sense Approach to Web Usability.* Indianapolis: Que Publishing, 2000.

Morgan, George G. *Your Family Reunion: How to Plan It, Organize It, and Enjoy It.* Orem, VT: Ancestry Publishing, 2001.

Platt, Lyman D. *Hispanic Surnames and Family History.* Baltimore: Genealogical Publishing, 1996.

Ptak, Diane Snyder. *Surnames: Their Meanings and Origins.* Self-published by Diane Ptak.

Schleifer, Jay. *A Student's Guide to Jewish American Genealogy.* Westport, CT: Greenwood Publishing, 1996.

She, Colleen. *A Student's Guide to Chinese American Genealogy.* Westport, CT: Greenwood Publishing, 1996.

Shea, Jonathan D., and William Hoffman. *Following the Paper Trail.* Bergenfield, NJ: Avotaynu, 1994.

Siegel, David. *Creating Killer Web Sites.* Indianapolis: Hayden Books, 1997.

Szucs, Loretto Dennis. *They Became Americans: Finding Naturalization Records and Ethnic Origins.* Orem, VT: Ancestry Publishing, 1998.

Thackery, David T. *Finding Your African American Ancestors.* Orem, VT: Ancestry Publishing, 2000.

Yamaguchi, Yoshi. *A Student's Guide to Japanese American Genealogy.* Westport, CT: Greenwood Publishing, 1996.

Magazines

The magazines listed below are available at large bookstores and some libraries. For more magazines, see http://www.cyndislist.com/magazines.htm

American History

Ancestry

Everton's Family History

Family Chronicle

Family History News (Canada)

Genealogical Computing

Most Popular Genealogy Software

Brothers Keeper, 6.0. Free download from http://www.bkwin.net.

Family Tree Maker, 9.0. Broderbund, $69.99.

Generations Family Tree. Sierra Home, $29.99.

Legacy 4.0. Free download from http://www.legacy.com.

Master Genealogist Silver Edition. Wholly Genes, $19.99.

Personal Ancestral File. Free download from http://www
.familysearch.org.

Reunion 7.0. Leister Productions for MacIntosh, $99.95.

Videos and CDS

Family History on the Internet, http://www.Ancestry.com.

Barbara Renick's Guide to Gen Info Online, http://www
.Ancestry.com.

List of Related Online Sites

African Ancestored Genealogy
http://www.afrigeneas.com
Genealogy resources for African-Americans.

SuperPages.com
http://www.bigbook.com
A yellow pages directory for the U.S.

Dead Fred: The Original Genealogy Photo Archive
http://www.deadfred.com
A collection of genealogy photos; includes genealogy news articles, surname listings, and mailing lists.

Federation of Eastern European Family History Societies
http://feefhs.org
A do-it-yourself destination answering questions related to East European genealogy.

UK and Ireland Genealogy
http://www.genuki.org.uk
A comprehensive site for British and Irish genealogy.

Archives in Germany
http://home.bawue.de/~hanacek/info/earchive.htm
Locations of records in Germany.

The Offical Home of Jewish Genealogy
http://www.jewishgen.org
Jewish and other immigrant ancestors.

Native American Genealogy
http://members.aol.com/bbbenge/front.html
Location of Native American records and resources.

Polish Genealogical Society of America
http://www.pgsa.org
Provides resources for research within the borders of the Old Commonwealth of Poland.

Canada GenWeb for Kids Project
http://www.rootsweb.com/~cangwkid/
Genealogy tips for Canadian kids and teens.

RootsWeb.com
http://searches.rootsweb.com
Worldwide database collected by RootsWeb volunteers.

Organizations

Association of Professional Genealogists
http://www.apgen.org

Canada's National History Society
http://www.historysociety.ca

General Society of *Mayflower* Descendants
http://www.mayflower.org

International Society of Sons and Daughters of Slave Ancestry
http://www.rootsweb.com/~ilissdsa

Italian Sons and Daughters of America
http://www.orderisda.org

National Genealogical Society
http://www.ngsgenealogy.org

National Japanese American Historical Society
http://www.nikkeiheritage.org

Sons of Norway
http://www.sofn.com

Index

U.S. Patent and Trademark
   Office, 39
U.S. presidents' families, 21

Veterans. *See* military and
   pension records

Web sites
   adoption.com, 58
   adoptionregistry.com, 58
   adoptionretriever.com, 58
   afrigeneas.com, 49, 70
   ancestry.com, 28, 47
   awesomeancestors.com,
      124–125
   ccharity.com, 70
   commercial, 28
   DearMyrtle.com, 124
   ellisislandrecords.org, 71
   familysearch.org, 45–46
   genealogy.com, 28
   genforum.genealogy.com,
      53–55
   gengateway.com, 49

hispanicgenealogy.com, 70
ireland.com, 70–71
italiangenealogy.com, 71
jewishgen.org, 70
legacyfamilytree.com, 21
people-finder Internet sites,
   67–68
reunite.com, 58
rootsweb.com, 40–45, 124
royalgenealogy.com, 21
usgenweb.org, 65–67
vitalchek.com, 78
vitalog.net, 47–48
worldgenweb.org, 65–67
West, Elisha Goodwin, *100*
Wilde, Candee, 13
William, Prince of England,
   12
wills. *See* probate or administration files
WorldGen Web Project, The,
   65–67

Zeveloff, Susannah, 11